BRITISH RAILWA

PAST and PRESENT

No 64

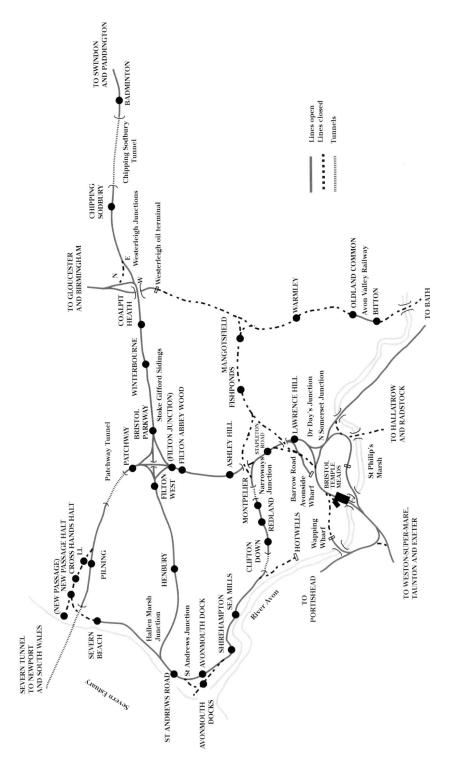

Map of the area covered by this book, showing locations featured or referred to in the text.

BRITISH RAILWAYS

PAST and PRESENT

No 64
Bristol and South Gloucestershire

John Stretton

Past & Present Publishing Ltd

First published in 2011

British Library Cataloguing in Publication Data

A catalogue record for this book is available from the British Library.

ISBN 978 1 85895 269 7

Past & Present Publishing Ltd
The Trundle
Ringstead Road
Great Addington
Kettering
Northants NN14 4BW

Tel/Fax: 01536 330588
email: sales@nostalgiacollection.com
Website: www.nostalgiacollection.com

Printed and bound in the Czech Republic

ACKNOWLEDGEMENTS

As with any project such as this, there are highs and lows. The latter usually come when you arrive at a promising location to find that the promise is frustrated and/or unfulfilled. The former, however, are thankfully more frequent and likely to derive from the material sent by the various contributors. Almost without exception, there are gems and the unexpected, and the arrival of each package is a source of anticipation and delight. For around 120 'past' photographic spaces I had in excess of 500 prints and colour slides! Again, as with others books that I have prepared, the projects would have been so much weaker without these ready and helpful supporters, especially those who have lent me their precious negatives, to produce best-quality images. Thus, without further hesitation, I thank all who have helped me, no matter how small the assistance. It has all been worth it, but there those who deserve especial mention. The photographers are credited with their work, but in addition, in no particular order, the following deserve truly grateful thanks for their help and support: Mike Mensing, Mike Goodfield, Tom Heavyside, Richard Casserley (as always, for his cooperation and patience!), Julian Crow, John Saville, Justin Hiscox, Dave Withers, John Chalcraft of www.railphotoprints. co.uk, Tim Maddocks and Ben Ashworth. Peter Townsend and David Walshaw at Silver Link and Will Adams of Keyword Ltd have all played their part in the production, with patience, never-failing courtesy and always with encouragement. Like a football team, one needs willing support. Thank you one and all!

Contents

BRISTOL (BATH ROAD) SHED: A delightful and near magical view of Bath Road shed in its incarnation as a diesel depot. During the night-time of 17 August 1963, the lights within and without (with their halos) witness the presence of several NBL Class 22s (D63xx), a 'Hymek' and a 'Peak'. The three-road 'Daily Shed' (centre) housed six locos between duties, with the main shed to its right undertaking B and C Exams. The signal box and offices – left and right – also have their interiors well illuminated. *Ben Ashworth*

BRISTOL TEMPLE MEADS (OLD): It is 11 minutes past midday on 3 October 1964 and No 82041 waits for the 'off' from Platform 14, watched by a father and his offspring at the rear of the loco. Station staff lean casually against the furniture, while sacks of mail are piled in the foreground on the ancient wooden platform. With Brunel's architecture, semaphore signals and large sign indicating the way to the 'new' station, the image is full of atmosphere that we all once took so much for granted. *Ben Ashworth*

Introduction

Since the first two volumes in this trilogy looking at the railways in Gloucestershire over the years – No 58 *North Gloucestershire* and No 59 *Central Gloucestershire* – appeared in 2008, I have been constantly asked when 'Volume 3' will be available. Well, here it is! I hope those that have waited with such patience will not be disappointed.

In total, the county is a sprawling and disparate animal, stretching far and wide and with the extremes of rural idyll and bustling, large cities. With the exception of Gloucester itself, the first of the two facets was the more visible feature in those earlier publications, whereas this time the city demands a greater part, with the heart and the tentacles of Bristol so pertinent. This does give a slightly different feel to this third selection, but the comparisons are none the less interesting and the history behind the city and the development of its railway network provide a vivid canvas on which to place our particular focus.

In steam days, Bristol and its surroundings was a very special place for railway enthusiasts. Not only was there Brunel's line to London, but there was also a route to Wales, the north-south axis running through Temple Meads, and the late-lamented 'by-pass' from Birmingham to Bath, via Mangotsfield. Mix in the heavily industrialised area around Avonmouth and there was – and still is – a lot to see and enjoy. Three large engine sheds once served the city and various routes, with healthy allocations, a bewildering array of motive power and vital work. Sadly, two of these have disappeared, Barrow Road from November 1965 and Bath Road, closed to steam very early, in September 1960, and more recently dispensed with completely. For those of us who knew the shed as an important part of the railway and Temple Meads scene, it is dispiriting to witness the current bare earth where the depot once stood so proudly.

Being a third volume of 'then and now' views of the county has given me the space and the opportunity to trawl for fresh shots and I have been fortunate to come up with many that, as far as I am aware, have not been seen in print before. As has been the case with previous Past and Present books that I have completed, it has been a joy visiting the 'old haunts' – though some have taken serious detective work to discover and to identify the footprints of the original photographers! – and the passage of time has meant that in some cases today's view is either meaningless or has been virtually impossible to access. As with other titles in this and similar series, there are occasions when the railway has all but disappeared from the scene, but happily there is still much to be seen on today's system within Gloucestershire's boundary and there are also areas where remnants of the previous existence are still extant, including such as Mangotsfield, where the infrastructure has been put to good modern use. Viewing all this variety has been part of the delight of the preparation of this volume and I hope that the disparate images will give satisfaction. In addition, I have occasionally broken the strict 'then and now' format to include illustrations that deserved to be seen on their own merits and I crave indulgence for this personal preference.

Steam and much else besides disappeared from the county over the years, but thankfully farsighted cameramen recorded much that was around prior to that, which now gives us both pleasure and a hankering for days gone by. Sadly, our present railway is often so much poorer in aesthetics, especially where infrastructure and signalling are concerned, but with the proliferation of liveries and new types of motive power since privatisation in 1994 there is at least some variety still to be had. The railway may be much changed, but for the photographer there is much to capture and the challenge is now even greater than of yore to create a satisfying image! It would be wonderful to see some stations and/or lines reopen, but this is 'pie in the sky' and wishful thinking in most instances; however, one can but dream! And there is a message there for our present-day photographers – the future will need the images that you could take today!

BADMINTON: A sight that once seemed so permanent. On 13 June 1959, Badminton station stands confidently astride the four-track London-Bristol main line as 'Britannia' No 70016 *Ariel* slowly pulls away from its stop at the station with the 1.55pm Paddington to Swansea ten-coach express, with the appropriate BR(W) code affixed to the smokebox front. New in July 1951, *Ariel* spent its first two years on the Eastern and North Eastern Regions, before working over Brunel's 'racetrack' between August 1953 and September 1961. *Hugh Ballantyne*

Badminton to the Severn Tunnel

BADMINTON: A second view of Badminton has us this time looking westwards towards Bristol. No 4079 *Pendennis Castle* was to become one of the most famous locomotives of its class, but is here seen in squadron service, on 22 November 1959, at speed on the through line, operating the 11.45am non-stop Bristol to Paddington express. Out of Works the previous month, the loco is obviously in fine fettle, on what was at the time one of the crack turns on BR's Western Region (BR[W]). Preservation came after withdrawal in 1964, but its subsequent history was turbulent and would fit well into a fictional story!

Opened on 1 July 1903, exactly 100 miles from Paddington and situated between Hullavington and Chipping Sodbury, and actually in Acton Turville, the station was named after the slightly more distant Great Badminton, with its large deer park; and it was only allowed on the Duke of Beaufort's land on condition that main-line trains stopped a stipulated number of times a day! The famed horse shows held there were the source of much business, with horses brought in by train far more easily than by way of the winding and narrow local country roads. This facility ceased when, despite much opposition, the station closed on 3 June 1968. As seen on 22 August 2010, the two station buildings are extant, but in a sad state of repair and heavily surrounded by tree growth. With No 66068 working a ballast train, it hardly seems conceivable that there was space for four tracks here! *Hugh Ballantyne/MJS*

CHIPPING SODBURY: Like Badminton, Chipping Sodbury station, just over 4 miles to the west, was opened on 1 July 1903 but, sadly, its tenure was not to be quite as long, closing on 3 April 1961. Just short of a mile west of the 4,433-yard-long eponymous tunnel, the station, on the Great Western main line (GWML), served both Chipping Sodbury and its near neighbour Yate, but the later population growth that has virtually joined the two places came too late to save it from pre-Beeching closure. As can be seen, housing was close by the line and the station was blessed with a goods shed, a full roster of traffic facilities and a 6-ton crane in the goods yard. On Friday 22 July 1983 No 45116 heads past with the 0935 Cardiff Central-Paddington service.

A slightly closer view, a few moments earlier on the same day, witnesses that the station building and the up platform are still in place, but the down-side infrastructure, to the left, has all gone. HST set No 253016 is in danger of completely losing its front identity as it forms the 0735 Carmarthen-Paddington express towards London. *Both John Acton, MJS collection*

CHIPPING SODBURY: Now to the west of the station, the bridge from which the views on the previous page were taken can be seen in the distance. On 30 August 1981 the up platform and building can be seen in closer focus, together with the coal yard and the curving sidings from the main line. Still in the days of loco-hauled passenger trains, No 47280 passes the station site with the 10.27 Paddington-Penzance service, here diverted via the Badminton route due to engineering work..

The current regime shows much change in the comparative view on 1 September 2010. An unidentified FGW-liveried HST set powers westwards as the 0815 Paddington-Cardiff Central express. Some of the up platform and its building have gone, as has all vestige of the previous coal yard and goods shed. One of the erstwhile sidings curving from the main line is still in place but is now more usually occupied by engineering machinery. Note that while the foliage to the left has spread upwards, the right-hand embankment has seen some clearance over the years. *John Chalcraft/MJS*

CHIPPING SODBURY: Down 'on the ground', in earlier times, father and son Henry and Richard Casserley pay a visit on 25 September 1960. Despite being during a period when the station was fully active, it has the impression of being rather 'down at heel', with the footbridge and the water crane showing the effects of being visited by steam engines, and the running-in board less than pristine!

While Dad was on the embankment, son Richard has ventured into the cess, to capture the view towards London. With the piles of new wooden sleepers alongside and the ladder in the four-foot, it is presumably during a time of engineering possession.

Moving to a position partway along what would have been the down platform, a collection of rail workers under instruction have just acknowledged the warning horn from the HST driver and stand clear of the line on 18 March 1997. No 43012 passes at around 120mph while forming the 1000 Paddington-Swansea express. *H. C. Casserley/Richard Casserley/MJS*

CHIPPING SODBURY: Turning through 180 degrees, and now looking towards Bristol from the end of the down platform, 'Hall' 4-6-0 No 4982 *Acton Hall* approaches on the through road with an up express for Paddington in around 1958. Close to its 30th birthday, it was still a resident of South Wales at this time, where it had spent many years, but would shortly begin wandering – to Tyseley, then Old Oak Common in February 1961 and Laira seven months later, from where the end came on 19 May 1962. The magnificent arched bridge is somewhat 'over the top', as it merely carries a footpath!

By the time of this comparative view, both the platform loop line and its attendant semaphore signal have gone, the latter replaced by the colour light gantry. On 18 March 1997 No 37154, looking rather grubby in its short-lived 'Transrail' livery, makes it way leisurely eastwards with a rake of loaded ballast wagons, ready for use under an engineer's possession. Note the heightened ballast shoulder compared to the 1958 view above, and how the embankment is now a forest of trees rather than the neat grass of yore.
John Chalcraft collection/MJS

WESTERLEIGH EAST: On 30 August 1959 No 5380 passes the now closed wartime-built Westerleigh East signal box with the 3.55pm (Sundays only) Swindon to Bristol Temple Meads local service. Opened on 1 July 1942, the box contained 44 levers and controlled the two loops and a total of 12 military sidings that were provided at the same time for Wapley Common Depot. The latter ceased to be rail-connected from May 1967, but the signal box remained functional until 10 May 1971. The view today has just the two main lines and is virtually unrecognisable. *Hugh Ballantyne*

WESTERLEIGH WEST JUNCTION: Roughly half a mile from East box, West Junction Box was positioned between the GWR main line in the foreground and the line from Bristol to the north. Using the latter, an unidentified 'Hall' 4-6-0 negotiates the curve as it hauls the 10.05am Saturdays-only ten-coach Kingswear to Wolverhampton holiday special on 14 August 1965. The box appears to have been recently repainted. *MJS*

WESTERLEIGH: A UK-based oil company founded in 1960, Murco Petroleum Ltd operates four refinery terminals, including the one at Westerleigh, at the southern end of what was once the through route to Bath, severed after closure by the M4 motorway. Daily services have used the site for many years, this view dating from 17 March 1997. Relatively new – entering service in March 1993 – No 60015 *Bow Fell* begins its journey as 6B25, the 1315 train to Robeston, with empty Murco tanks. To the left, No 60034 *Carnedd Llewelyn* waits to follow with an extra load. The terminal stands at the foot of the embankment seen in the distance.

Moving forward 13½ years, the Class 60s are still in charge, but for how much longer is uncertain, for at the time of the photograph DB, now the operator of the EWS stock, threatened to withdraw the entire class from service, but subsequently had a change of policy, with a proposal to upgrade a number of the class to 'Super 60s'. Escaping the reliverying of the past few years, two-tone-grey No 60084 starts 6E41, the 1141 Westerleigh-Lindsey empty bogie oil tanks, from the oil terminal on Wednesday 1 September 2010. Having been in store, this loco had only just been returned to service, ready for the leaf-fall season. *Both MJS*

WINTERBOURNE VIADUCT: In a magnificent vista and delightful scene, a diminutive train set crosses the viaduct on 20 September 1964. Though carrying the GWR main line, the structure, with its height and slender piers, gives the impression of being rather flimsy for the task. Returning from Bristol to Swindon, No 1444 trundles over the valley with its two coaches full of enthusiasts from the Great Western Society, who have been out for the day visiting various lines in the locality, including the Calne branch. *Hugh Ballantyne*

WINTERBOURNE station was another on the line that lasted for a little over half a century, closing, with Chipping Sodbury, on 3 April 1961. Looking towards London, the 269-yard-long Huckford (aka Hackford) Viaduct is framed by the still extant covered footbridge, despite the station now obviously closed in this undated view. Work has begun on dismantling, with platform edging slabs removed and the station name no longer in place. Somewhat strangely, the goods yard, behind the photographer in this view, remained open until 7 October 1963! *Colour-Rail collection*

STOKE GIFFORD: The Parish of Stoke Gifford extends eastwards to Winterbourne, and it joined the railway network in 1903, at the same time as the locations we have already seen. Although graced with sidings from the start, five extra ones were added both north and south of the main running line in 1918, to cope with increasing traffic. This view on 9 May 1964, from the footbridge to the east of the site, shows just how this extension widely opened the land area occupied by the tracks. At this time the expanse was just a very busy goods yard, with the arrival of a station here still eight years ahead. The East signal box, with 31 levers, is visible between the two left-hand running lines.

By 18 April 1980, the date of this view, the relatively new Bristol Parkway – opened on 1 July 1972 with minimal facilities and no platform cover – stands in the distance, with its initial concept design of two fairly basic platforms. Many of the sidings have disappeared, especially to the right, where a sparsely occupied free car park has taken residence. An 11-coach train, the norm of the day, is loco-hauled by No 47544, forming the 0747 Penzance-Liverpool (Lime Street) cross-country service. The East signal box and the ex-GWR water tank are conspicuous by their absence. *P. J. Garland, Roger Carpenter collection/John Acton, MJS collection*

BRISTOL PARKWAY: Twenty-one years later the vista has changed yet again. To the left of the running lines the sidings are as before, with just the addition of a new signal, lighting towers and speed restriction sign, but on the other the situation is vastly altered. This end of the former car park has been subsumed beneath a new Royal Mail hub, which has had sidings realigned to accommodate an island platform. Foliage has grown apace but the church tower is still just visible. On 5 May 2001 the then brand-new 'Voyager' No 220003 leaves the station with a 5Z11 Plymouth-Central Rivers test train, resplendent in its Virgin livery.

A further nine years on and there is yet more change in certain areas. To the left, all is largely as before, with the exception of more greenery, but on the right events and reappraisals have again forced transformation. The Royal Mail facility – only in use until January 2004! – and its attendant 'station' have disappeared, to be replaced by a building for a Network Rail Training School and, now, a two-tier parking area, although this is hidden from view by tree growth. On 22 August 2010 'Voyagers' are now very much part of the scenery, though now in the CrossCountry coat that superseded the Virgin look, as an unidentified member of the type approaches Parkway forming the 1212 Birmingham New Street-Plymouth service. *Both MJS*

BRISTOL PARKWAY: On the platform on 12 March 1981, the growth of business over the eight years since opening is evidenced by the now well-populated car park on the right and rudimentary shelters erected over the platforms. As can be seen from this view, however, these gave very little practical protection from the elements! No 43035, at this end of the 1015 Paddington-Swansea service, is surprisingly standing in the up platform, having been diverted via Bath due to flooding in Chipping Sodbury Tunnel after heavy rain storms.

On 22 August 2010 the 'wrong line' situation is repeated, though this time due to weekend engineering possession around the Chipping Sodbury area, as No 43125 waits to travel into Wales from the up road. The more roundabout route via Bath had caused delay to the service, but this was exacerbated on this day by signal failure problems at Stapleton Road, just to the north of Bristol Temple Meads. The tree to the left takes away some of the harshness of the station ambience and there is a new shelter on the up platform, together with a third platform face, to the right, to accommodate further growth in demand. Note the two-tier car park beyond. *John Acton, MJS collection/MJS*

BRISTOL PARKWAY: At the western end of the station on 11 June 1978 Swindon-built DMU set No C509 enters with a service from Cardiff. The initial squat, ground-level station building is seen to the right of the train, together with the rather utilitarian, low-cost architecture of the footbridge. At least the clocks are roughly in sync, even if the second hands do not agree!

By 18 April 1980 nothing has changed structurally, but the motive power is somewhat stronger! No 46001 runs into the station and prepares to stop as the 0747 Penzance-Liverpool Lime Street cross-country express. A development of the Class 45s, the former D138 of 1961 was stored just six months after this view, then withdrawn in December, before being reinstated in September 1981 and discarded again three months later. Its fate was to be dismemberment at Swindon Works in July 1982.

After the passage of a further 30 years there is now much greater change. The track and platforms are the same, but elsewhere the positioning of the steps access to the platforms and the attendant footbridge are further east, together with the redesign of the main station building. The ground-level entrance is in a new, purpose-built structure, with access to the platforms under cover of the sweeping canopy; even the colour-

light gantry at the western end of the platform has seen redesign. On 22 August 2010 'double-headed' single cars Nos 153370 and 153369 roll into the station with the 1241 Bristol Temple Meads-Worcester Shrub Hill local service, 1 hour late due to a signal failure at Stapleton Rd, and due to be truncated at Cheltenham; passengers for Ashchurch and Worcester were then to be ferried by road. *Colour-Rail collection/ John Acton, MJS collection/MJS*

BRISTOL PARKWAY: The present-day futuristic station and the land that it now occupies in the erstwhile Stoke Gifford goods yard are readily apparent in this view from 11 September 2010. The sun shines brightly on an unusually quiet scene, caused by weekend closure due to engineering work to the junction layout immediately west of the station; on the right, No 66506 is temporarily marooned with its rake of coal wagons until the end of this phase of the work on the Monday morning.

Swinging through 180 degrees, we are now looking west to see some of the work involved. The weekend of 11/12 September 2010 was the first of four weekend possessions to renovate part of the intensively used layout. On Saturday 11th, the view shows new panels put into place, awaiting ballast, with a road/rail machine ready and waiting and No 66168 at the head of a rake of empty wagons to collect spent ballast from the excavation under way on the other side of the train. Note the compulsory 'hi-vis' apparel and helmets compared to past practice. *Both MJS*

PATCHWAY: From Badminton to Patchway the line is virtually a continuous falling 1 in 300 gradient, with just two very short level stretches between Chipping Sodbury Tunnel and station, and at Bristol Parkway. Patchway station is also on the level, before another stretch of down gradient. On 5 August 1988 two-car DMU set No 155307 – less than a year old – runs into the station forming the 1510 Portsmouth Harbour-Cardiff Central service. Like most of this Leyland type, it was split into two Class 153 units in February 1992, becoming Nos 153307 and 153357. Note the wide open vista … and the man waving from the skeletal scaffold atop the squat building beyond the rear coach!

The same vantage point, the same waiting shelter – with a new warning sign – and the same lamp standard – now adorned with a platform number – but the view is now constricted and contained by arboreal growth over the two decades. On 22 August 2010 FGW-liveried HST No 43137 sweeps into the station – not stopping, however – as the 1130 Paddington-Carmarthen service, delayed both by engineering work in the Chipping Sodbury area and a signal failure at Stapleton Road. *Mike Mensing/MJS*

PATCHWAY: The climb from the Severn Tunnel eastwards was ever a tough challenge for steam locomotives, with the up entrance to the station on the level being a relief after the climb at 1 in 100. The down slope can be seen to the rear of the mixed 'express' goods entering the station behind No 3406 *Calcutta* early in 1948. Allocated to Didcot when seen, it was withdrawn in May of that year. Note the platform-end signals on the left and the attractive trees to the right, giving a country feel to the station.

The view from the footbridge at 19.42 on 2 June 1982 still shows a rural aspect, but the trees have gone, as have the signals. The down gradient is again obvious at the rear of an up ten-coach special in connection with Pope John Paul's visit to the UK, hauled by No 47121. Looking in smart condition, the 47 was one of the relatively few to retain its original TOPS number and not to be renumbered. It was named *Pochard* – unofficially at Tinsley depot in December 1989, then officially at Old Oak Common in April 1994! – before being withdrawn from Stratford on 24 September 1996.

By 22 August 2010 trees have grown but, sadly, they are unable to retain the rural feel, following the spread of Bristol into previous spacious green areas. Piles of waste paper and wood now inhabit the space between the station and Station Road that once held a long siding passing under the distant bridge. HST power car No 43004 trails the 1130 Paddington-Carmarthen service, another one delayed by engineering work in the Chipping Sodbury area and the signal failure at Stapleton Road. *Frank Robertshaw collection/Mike Mensing/MJS*

PATCHWAY: Emerging from the station in the post-war, early-nationalisation period, an unidentified 'Hall' heads west at around 19.49 with a Portsmouth-Cardiff express that includes ex-SR stock. The graceful, stately trees still overlook the scene, with some counter-balance provided by the ringed signal gantry to the right, protecting trains waiting to leave the 1905 down goods loop. The long up siding is graced with similar provision. Note the covered footbridge.

Moving further westwards on an unidentified date, but probably 1964 when the locomotive was allocated to 86B between May and its November withdrawal, No 4233 runs away from the now treeless station light engine on its way through to Severn Tunnel Junction and back home to Newport. Station Road and the long siding are clearly seen here, while to the right a coal train awaits its turn to leave the loop and join the main line.

The comparative view on 4 May 1983 shows that the long siding has been dispensed with, as has, in the distance, the down loop and the footbridge's covering. The semaphore signals have also disappeared, to be replaced by a lesser number of colour lights. Steam has been absent from this scene for nearly 20 years as we see double-headed Class 25s Nos 25054 and 25064 hauling a Cranmore-Ellesmere Port empty tanks train, which will travel via the Severn Tunnel and the Welsh Marches route to Cheshire.

Today there is no evidence of the long up siding, taken out of use from 5 May 1968; the open fields to the left are now obscured by trees; the shallow embankment on the right has been totally colonised by nature; and Station Road is hidden by more industrial waste. On 1 September 2010 No 43027 speeds through the station at the head of the 1045 Paddington-Swansea express. *Roger Carpenter collection/Paul Chancellor collection/Tom Heavyside/MJS*

PATCHWAY: West of the footbridge from which the last four views were taken, the up and down lines separate at different levels. The former climbs up to the station for nearly 3 miles at 1 in 100, and No 2844 can be seen working hard in 1936, with its cargo of private-owner wagons containing a variety of items, including anthracite in the leading vehicle. Note the two ladies out walking along Station Road with a pram, and the long up refuge siding running to its buffer stops.

By 18 April 1980 the alignment of that long siding is still visible but it has been slightly narrowed following attention to the embankment. No 253029 climbs towards the level forming the 1345 Swansea-Paddington express, while the track to the left is still level but about to suddenly dive down at 1 in 90.

'…and I'll tak' the low road!' On Wednesday 1 September 2010 No 43147 climbs from the nearby tunnel towards Patchway as the 1155 Cardiff Central-Paddington express. Again, tree growth has resculptured the landscape and, to the right, has conspired with encroaching development to totally disguise the former long siding alignment. *Frank Robertshaw collection/John Acton, MJS collection/MJS*

PATCHWAY: The bridge seen on the extreme upper left of the shot of No 253029 opposite was, in times past, a superb vantage point for the 1,762-yard Patchway New Tunnel. In steam days, despite the vent that can be seen on the hilltop, smoke was a real problem as the trains climbed the 1-mile 1 in 100 gradient, but even in more recent times conditions could still be tough. On 4 May 1983 it is a mixture of diesel exhaust and coal dust that slowly pours from the tunnel mouth, rather than smoke and steam, as No 47098 heads an up train, quite possibly bound for Didcot Power Station.

The construction of a new road locally and the erection by Network Rail of palisade fencing around the railway's land, leading to the creation of a new foot underpass to the road, prevents a precise recreation. Thus this view is slightly to the right, to show No 43012 speeding out of the tunnel with the 1128 Swansea-Paddington express on 1 September 2010. There are no obvious emissions from the tunnel mouth and there is no change to the basic layout. There is now fencing alongside the upper line, which falls at 1 in 90 and was formerly the single-line route from Patchway to New Passage, between 1863 and 1886. Nature is being controlled along the embankments but is increasing above, concealing the newer buildings beyond. *Tom Heavyside/MJS*

PILNING: Just short of 4 miles from Patchway, Pilning (High Level) was the last station on the London-South Wales main line before it plunged into the darkness beneath the Severn Estuary. With a rail link to the Low Level station, the access road for which can be seen on the extreme left, sidings, a full range of customer services and a 1 ton 10 cwt crane, in addition to the main-line trains, the station was a busy place at its height. On 14 July 1958 No 6834 *Dummer Grange* hurries west along the main line with a mixed freight, as No 4127 and coach W6466W on the left, operating as the 4.40pm service from Severn Tunnel Junction to Bristol, sets back to offload the photographer's 1934 Hillman Minx, registration JY 4711.

A slightly later view shows the site largely unchanged, apart from the addition of a sign on the up-side concrete lamp post indicating where six-car DMUs should stop. The 1905 down loop is again filled with a goods train that will

recommence its journey after the passage of the unidentified 'Britannia' with 'The Red Dragon' express. The bay to the left was used for some years to house the Tunnel emergency train.

Until the opening of the Severn Bridge in 1966, carrying the M4 motorway into Wales, Pilning was a popular station for Bristolians to drive to in order to catch a train into Wales, as there was good parking and a regular service. This no longer happens and, though still open, it has just one train a week, a Saturdays-only 'Parliamentary' service, to Cardiff and Taunton. The site has been drastically remodelled, with only the 1905 loop still in place alongside the main line. On 1 September 2010 an unidentified HST set has no intention of stopping as it approaches with the 1215 Paddington-Cardiff Central express. *H. C. Casserley/ MJS collection/MJS*

PILNING: Opened on 1 December 1886, the new structure replaced that on the 1863 branch to New Passage, which was initially single track. A second line was completed in May 1887, approached from the east on the level for about half a mile before falling at 1 in 636 through the platforms, then more steeply at 1 in 100 to the Severn Tunnel. By the date of this view, 28 April 1973, the station received just one train per day and the station buildings were boarded up, as can be seen, as a group of enthusiasts visit to take in the view before the old order is swept away.

By 6 January 1982, as No 47090 hurries past with an up van train, only the brick building remains from the earlier view, now in the possession of BR engineers. The station ceased to be known as 'High Level' from 1966 and the truncated name can be seen on the more modern station nameboard affixed to the lamp standard on the right. A new, basic waiting shelter has been provided on the down platform on the left.

An electricity pylon has materialised by 1 September 2010; the waiting shelter has been 'modernised'; the brick building has seen brickwork renewed and the windows reopened; and a new building has appeared alongside. The 1906 up loop – seen beyond the rear carriage – still serves, but lighting has disappeared from the platforms. DMU No 158957 is working another non-stop service through the station, the 1330 Cardiff Central-Portsmouth Harbour semi-fast. *John Edgington/John Acton, MJS collection/MJS*

PILNING: A glorious vision of GWR power at its height! 'King' No 6019 *King Henry V* breasts the climb from the Severn Tunnel and one can almost hear and feel the demonstration of effort as it storms through the station on 10 February 1962 at the head of the 8.00am Neyland-Paddington express. The running-in board advertises local services, which could be had from the adjacent Low Level station. These ceased when the branch to Avonmouth, via New Passage and Severn Beach, was closed from 23 November 1964. Despite the outward appearance of the loco and this being a 'top link' duty, the writing was on the wall for the 'King' Class, and *Henry V* lost his battle for life just seven months after this view, on 8 September, from Wolverhampton Stafford Road shed.

Captured at the same spot, in glorious late-summer sunshine, No 43149 roars into Pilning station on Wednesday 1 September 2010 with the 1228 Swansea-Paddington express, but the excitement is not the same! There is no sense of motion, nor yet emotion, as the supremely able and effective motive power simply takes the climb in its stride. Gone are all the fittings associated with the steam era, leaving a denuded station, and no amount of foliage can dispel the sense of desertion here. *Hugh Ballantyne/MJS*

PILNING (LOW LEVEL): The single line from Severn Beach to Pilning, utilising the old branch from New Passage, was opened on 5 February 1900, but it did not have its own station here until 1928. Cheek-by-jowl with its larger neighbour, Low Level did, nevertheless, have four sidings, fanning in the platform area from the single-line junction with the main line. Some of these can be seen in this view of the station from the Hugh Level in 1930. Though a delightful setting, there were no waiting facilities here.

Nearly 20 years later, viewed from the approach to High Level, the station has new lighting, a waiting shelter and the words 'Low Level' added to the name board. The beginning of the sidings can be seen more clearly from this angle, as can the signal protecting the exit eastwards towards the main line.

With the two past vantage points now obliterated by trees, this is the station site looking west along the alignment of the old trackbed. The platform was to the right and the sidings occupying much of the left-hand side of the field, as seen on 1 September 2010. The distant pylon is that seen on the previous page. *Frank Robertshaw collection/P. J. Garland, Roger Carpenter collection/MJS*

31

CROSS HANDS HALT, a mile north-west of Pilning, was one of the very few stations in the UK to share its name with a nearby pub! As can be seen, it was surrounded by open space and the potential for business must have been low. The GWR had allowed for eventual double track, but this never transpired and the route remained both single and 'sleepy' throughout. Looking towards Pilning, No 82001 is relatively modern motive power for this isolated branch line, as it trundles along the final approach to Cross Hands with the 5.20pm Bristol Temple Meads-Severn Breach stopper on 9 May 1958. Note that the track and ballast have received some recent attention and renewal. By 2010, all that can be seen from this vantage point from the B4055 road is a wall of trees and undergrowth, with little to discern even the immediate trajectory. *Mike Mensing*

NEW PASSAGE: The terminus of the single-line branch from Patchway to New Passage Pier from 1863 to 1886 was to the north-east of the location pictured here. Located before the terminus, the newer station sat on what became a through route when connection was made south-westwards towards Severn Beach and Avonmouth in 1900. Closure came in November 1964. The station was always on a single line, like its neighbour Cross Hands half a mile away, and again there is absolutely no evidence of there ever having been a railway here. The house on the left, seen in around 1960 as the DMU heads for Severn Beach, has gone, and the site of the station is now buried under the new M4 on its way to the second Severn Bridge. *MJS collection*

SEVERN TUNNEL: Back on the main line to South Wales, No 70016 *Ariel* – seen earlier at Badminton – emerges from the 97-yard Ableton Lane Tunnel on 9 May 1958, shortly after passing through the Severn Tunnel, with the 12-coach 7.50am Fishguard Harbour-Paddington express. To the left is the 1942 extension of the 1905 loop that ran through Pilning, more than a mile further east! The right-hand goods line was installed at the same time. Note the hand-holds in the smoke deflectors, a trademark of the BR(W)-allocated 'Britannias'. Here allocated to Cardiff Canton shed, it departed from its Welsh homeland in 1961 and spent the rest of its career, until withdrawal in September 1967, travelling up and down the West Coast Main Line.

With Wales in the distance, on-loan EWS-liveried Nos 67028 and 67019 top-and-tail 2C79, the 1400 Cardiff-Taunton service, as it makes that same climb away from the Severn Tunnel and heads towards Pilning on Wednesday 1 September 2010. Since the early years of the 21st century the left-hand goods loop has been truncated, with access back to the main line now set a little further east; a colour-light gantry that stood adjacent to where No 67029 is pictured, has been removed; and access to the site for engineer's machines is in place to the right. The two crossovers to the rear of the train were installed in around 1989. *Mike Mensing/MJS*

Severn Beach to Montpelier

SEVERN BEACH: The railway came to Severn Beach in 1900, with the opening of the line from Avonmouth to Pilning, but initially it was merely a freight line; passenger services and a station were only provided in 1922, when there was little else for the visitor than estuary mud and predominantly western 'breezes'! The station buildings, erected in 1924 with a grandiose sheltered concourse, were at 90 degrees to the running line, perhaps as the passenger services from Bristol terminated here until 1928, when they were finally extended to Pilning. That extended route passed immediately behind the station sign to the left in this view. After closure of this link in 1964, the building stood empty for many years, and is seen here gated and boarded on Saturday 11 May 1985.

Subsequently demolished, a private house was erected, leaving the present station with no building at all. With that house on the right in this 1 September 2010 view, the old running line was immediately to the left of the current station sign. The now single-faced platform is straight ahead, with just a small shelter to protect visitors from the elements. *Mike Mensing/MJS*

SEVERN BEACH: The view looking towards Bristol in the pouring rain of August 1956 shows the two platform faces of the station, the right-hand one effectively a bay and the left-hand one as the through line. To the left, the twin sidings were predominantly for coach storage, although nominally freight services did survive until 10 June 1963. Note the ad-hoc power supply for the platform lighting!

Twenty-six years later there has been progress of sorts! The station survives, with tracks on both sides of the platform, but the 'bay' line has been shortened and the platform has lost all of its previous fittings. It is not exactly the most welcome of places on 27 April 1982, despite the ten passengers enjoying some spring sunshine as they decamp from DMU set No B804, forming the 1553 service from Bristol.

Through another 28 years there have been

more changes. All the track to the left has gone; the sole remaining line has now been lengthened slightly towards the buffers; and lighting and a small shelter have returned to the platform. On 1 September 2010 the service is still DMU-operated, this time by No 143619, a two-car set now in its 26th year and of the 'Pacer' type not universally loved (!), forming the 1554 service to Bristol Temple Meads. *H. C. Casserley/Tom Heavyside/MJS*

SEVERN BEACH: A busy time for once! The 2.12pm service from Bristol Temple Meads via Pilning waits to leave Beach station as the 3.00pm to Temple Meads via Clifton Down, to complete the circular journey on 28 September 1959. Having crossed the road in the background, the gates are closed behind the attractive-looking three-car WR Suburban DMU. Carriages wait for custom on the left, while another rake is between duties in one of the sidings.

Another view from 27 April 1982 again shows the naked appearance of the platform at this date. To the left, single-car DMU No W55033 waits to form the 1724 service to Bristol Temple Meads, while No 31294 makes a welcome visual change, as locomotives were highly unusual after the 1964 closure – apart from those serving ICI's Severnside Works – until 23 March 1992. Mike Goodfield, a contributor this volume, stands by the door of the Class 31, about to be relieved by another crew. With buffer stops rather than crossing gates in the background, the engine has just completed the run-round of its short train and prepares to head back to Bristol. The station was unstaffed from 1967, after a decline in the popularity of the resort with holidaymakers.

The view on 1 September 2010 shows further developments: there is a new station sign, no track to the right, the ex-BR 'double arrow' sign at the end of the station, and some attempt to brighten the ambience with raised flower beds made from old sleepers. Once again, No 143619 is seen forming the 1554 service to Bristol Temple Meads. *Mike Mensing/ Tom Heavyside/MJS*

SEVERN BEACH: In our last look at this location, on 27 April 1982 DMU No B804 (the B indicating Bristol area), with coach W51452 leading, waits patiently to become the 1645 service to Bristol Temple Meads, with the photographer grateful that he is not being subjected to inclement weather! New in June 1959, the leading coach was withdrawn in August 1987 and scrapped at Mayer Newman's site in Snailwell.

Managing to attract custom in the mid-afternoon sunshine, No 143619 is again seen waiting at Severn Beach on 1 September 2010, shortly to leave as the 1554 service to Bristol Temple Meads. The turnaround times at this terminus are very short indeed. New in January 1986, this unit came into being as No B804 above was reaching the end of its life. Note the housing in the background, taking advantage of the release of railway land. *Tom Heavyside/MJS*

ST ANDREWS ROAD: In the 1930s this view would have shown clean platforms with largely open fields on either side of the station. By 8 March 1960 how things have changed! Progressive developments of need and ideas through the Second World War and beyond took hold, to the extent that by the end of the 1960s the area was well and truly industrialised. The number and layout of the surrounding sidings have constantly changed, as has the supporting infrastructure, including pipes, overhead structures and, more recently, hoppers and conveyor belts. The station has never been overstretched, as can be judged by single-car No W55033 departing with the 1222 Severn Beach-Bristol Temple Meads service.

In the later years of the 20th century the up platform, from which W55033 was leaving, was dispensed with, to give more space for sidings to serve the various local needs. Still looking north but standing closer to the station footbridge, No 66162 is seen enjoying a rest over the weekend as it stands with its rake of empty coal hoppers on Saturday 11 September 2010. The sole remaining passenger track is that to the left, with the other lines leading to feed the hopper at the south end of the station. *Mike Mensing/MJS*

ST ANDREWS JUNCTION: Approximately half a mile south of the station, the route to Avonmouth crossed a level crossing controlled by St Andrews Junction Signal Box. On Saturday 11 May 1985 – two days before a revised timetable came into force – Class 121 DMU No W55026 crosses the road as the 1445 Bristol Temple Meads-Severn Beach local service and slows to accept something from the signalman. Looking rather akin to a block of wood, it can hardly have been a token, and the photographer wondered if it was, indeed, a copy of the revised timetable. Opened in 1910, the box looks as though it has recently received more than just a lick of paint.

With the railway's erstwhile passage through to Avonmouth now blocked by the massive improvised buffer stop (!), the comparative view is taken from the northern end of the box. Still serving its original function, since 1988 it has also been home to a satellite panel controlling other areas whose boxes have closed; it looks fine in its pseudo-GWR brown and cream coating on 11 September 2010. *Mike Mensing/MJS*

GLOUCESTER ROAD, AVONMOUTH DOCKS: Prior to 1903 the line from Bristol to Pilning, opened three years earlier, ran further west parallel with Avonmouth Dock and across Gloucester Road before curving north to reach St Andrews Junction. Viewed from the footbridge over the road, No 6671 receives clearance to travel south with its long and very mixed load on 26 August 1956 and approaches the site of the old Avonmouth Docks station, open from 1910 to 1915. The train is on one side of a triangular junction, with the left arm splitting to go along two sides of Royal Edward Dock and the third arm passing behind the Mountstuart Dry Docks Ltd building. *H. C. Casserley*

AVONMOUTH DOCK: The GWR & Midland Joint Avonmouth Dock station opened in 1883, at the end of a branch that subsequently became the through route to Pilning in 1900. The sharp curve in the distance is from St Andrews Junction, and the line now runs straight into the station, behind the photographer. In February 1959 a relatively new three-car DMU set bound for Bristol Temple Meads approaches the level crossing outside the station. It is a truly industrial scene redolent of the 19th century, with large factories, large chimneys and coal-burning terraced houses for the workers, which here look to be well cared for. To the left there had been two carriage sidings between 1924 and 1957.

The station footbridge has since disappeared and the comparative view is taken from the end of the down platform. The line to St Andrews Junction is now single, as it is all the way to Severn Beach, and the ugly flour mill and the terraced housing have been joined by more modern structures, including a wind turbine. 'Pacer' unit No 143611 drifts towards the station with the 1354 Severn Beach-Bristol Temple Meads service on Friday 3 September 2010. *MJS collection/MJS*

AVONMOUTH DOCK: In another view of a station shortly after a downpour, looking towards Bristol on 26 August 1956, ex-GWR 0-6-0PT No 7794 pauses by the canopy on Platform 2 with the 4.28pm train to Bristol via Henbury, its train doors open to accept its next customers. The crossover alongside was to allow a loco to run round its train, as not all services completed the journey to Severn Beach. To the left, a car stands by the station entrance, with the ticket barrier under cover and, beyond, an old-style garage, with just one pump, advertising a taxi hire facility. Note, to the right, the original station building, dating from 1926, as a replacement of an earlier, much more basic wooden shelter.

Five years later, on 4 March 1961, nothing has changed, on or off the railway, but it is looking very neat and tidy. Just visible at the far end of Platform 2, the 1903 signal box sits squat on the platform, its 36 levers controlling the main line and the siding behind the platform to the right.

The ensuing four decades have seen a change of fortunes for both the station and its traffic. By 3 September 2010 trains no longer run through to Pilning, the running-in board has gone, a small fence protects the platform slope and, more dramatically but out of shot, Platform 2 has lost its signal box and all its passenger facilities bar one small waiting shelter. The original building still stands, but in private hands. *Richard Casserley/ Edwin Wilmshurst/MJS*

AVONMOUTH DOCK: The aforementioned wooden shelter on Platform 2 is seen here in around 1913, from a position between the level crossing and the signal box. Out of sight to the left was a long bay platform, in use between 1903 and 1966, and to the right the large trees make a delightful border for the railway. Sadly, these had to be removed when the up platform was built in 1918. This train seems to be doing a roaring trade!

Crossing over to the 1918 platform on 26 August 1956, the layout of Platform 2 is seen in greater detail, including the bay platform with its own canopy. Initially closed in 1966, it was briefly reopened between 1971 and 1987 for use by Rowntree Mackintosh. Note the Gents' toilet block at this end of the main building.

The waiting shelter on Platform 1 is still extant, but the provision on No 2 is now very sparse, as is obvious on 3 September 2010. Also, it is clear that the near (Bristol) ends of the platforms are no longer in use, as at most times the maximum train length will be just two cars! The full-width crossing

gates in the background of the 1956 picture are now replaced with lifting barriers. *Lens of Sutton collection/Richard Casserley/MJS*

SHIREHAMPTON, opened in March 1865, had at its height two through lines with a crossover, and four sidings in a large goods yard that boasted a weighing machine. The fourth siding was installed in 1921 and extended across a road to access Nott Brodie & Co's yard; this lasted in situ until 1985. The 20-lever signal box sits on the down platform in this undated view, with housing on Dursley Road in the background.

The line was singled in 1970 – after staffing had been withdrawn three years earlier – and the down platform, signal box and track were removed and the ground left to nature. Thus the view on 3 September 2010 has a far more claustrophobic feel than the earlier one. Some of the Dursley Road houses can just be seen through the trees. *David Lawrence, Hugh Davies collection, MJS collection/MJS*

SEA MILLS: In its heyday, with the River Avon alongside and River Trym flowing into it under the short viaduct at the northern platform end, the station was a haven of peace and tranquillity. Some of that can be felt in this view from 26 August 1956 , with fields in the distance and foliage to the left, as the station is captured by the photographer from his train. As with Shirehampton, it was opened on 6 March 1865, as part of the Bristol Port Railway & Pier route from Hotwells to a deep-water pier on the Severn Estuary at Avonmouth. The line was diverted in 1885 and extended to run via Clifton Downs Tunnel to Bristol Temple Meads. The down platform was added in 1907, a year after the attractive station building was completed, and can just be seen beyond the end of the train. The locomotive is No 5559, hauling the 11.00am Bristol Temple Meads-Avonmouth service, and running wrong line due to engineering work.

Forty years of being abandoned to nature shows what can happen, as the down platform is completely smothered by buddleias, brambles, bushes and trees. The 1906 building can still be seen on 3 September 2010, now in private use and partly hidden by a newer waiting shelter. Note how tree growth has hidden the far fields. *Richard Casserley/MJS*

45

CLIFTON DOWN: Sea Mills may only be 2 miles from Clifton Down, but the latter is now well and truly part of suburban Bristol. When opened on 1 October 1874, as a terminus, trains of both the GWR and the Midland Railway – from Bristol Temple Meads and Mangotsfield respectively – brought custom, and grand buildings surrounded the location. Over the years it was also a Mecca for visitors to Bristol Zoo. It had a healthy goods traffic, and through trains to Sea Mills and beyond began on 1 September 1885. In this undated view from around 1956, a Class '57xx' 0-6-0PT restarts its journey from Temple Meads to Severn Beach. Note the extensive goods yard and 5-ton crane.

A view of two halves! To the right, the goods yard – closed on 5 July 1965 – has disappeared under new development, whereas the layout on the left-hand side is as before, although softened by greenery. The attractively designed and Grade II-listed station building is now a bar, but the once decorative canopies have disappeared, removed at different times between the 1930s and 1971. *MJS collection/MJS*

CLIFTON DOWN: A slightly longer train than normal is being hauled by a larger tank that usually seen on the branch, and the travellers waiting for its arrival could perhaps indicate that the working is a special to take trippers to Severn Beach. In this undated view, the canopy on the down platform is still in place, but the up platform has lost its version. Note the wide platform, a legacy of its time as a terminus when large numbers of passengers may have needed to be accommodated.

Moving across to the up platform, another arrival enters the station. On 6 May 1983 Class 121 No W55026 slows for the stop in the now denuded down platform with the 1808 Bristol Temple Meads-Severn Beach service. New in October 1960, from Pressed Steel, it lasted in squadron service until September 1992, after which it was converted to Departmental work as No 977824. Note that, with the splendid covered footbridge gone, the old entrance to the station has been blocked up, with a newer access under the 'tunnel' beyond the unit.

The comparative view on 3 September 2010 shows that the entrance has been reopened and connected to a newly erected footbridge. A new waiting shelter is on Platform 2 and the addition of a flower bed has served to soften the spartan image. 'Pacer' No 143620 enters with the 1516 Bristol Temple Meads-Severn Beach local service. A new barrier has been erected to prevent straying into the gloom under the building! Note that a new vent has been built into the wall of that building and, somehow, someone has managed to etch 'I.R.A.' alongside! *David Lawrence, Hugh Davies collection, MJS collection/Mike Mensing/MJS*

CLIFTON DOWN: Glancing back towards Severn Beach, this 1956 view from a train evidences the magnificently graceful and decorative ironwork of Platform 2's canopy. There are no doubts as to the whereabouts and nature of the various rooms and the original 1874 stonework adds its own charm. There was obviously a pride in the station's creation, though whether the originators would have approved of the 'Brylcreem' advert is arguable.

There is not the same feel without the canopy, but at least the Grade II building is being cared for and still looks attractive on 3 September 2010. At the end of the platforms the line runs straight into the 1,751-yard Clifton Down Tunnel. The murals now present in the erstwhile doorways and windows were the work of students at the North Bristol Post 16 Centre at the Redland Green Learning Community, as part of an art and design course and to promote links with Bristol Zoo. *H. C. Casserley/MJS*

REDLAND: No station was provided when the line first opened, and it was not until 12 years later, on 12 April 1897, that one appeared, after petitioning by local residents, with access from Redland Grove, behind the photographer. Initially with two platforms and buildings on both, the line was singled in the early 1970s and the buildings on the down platform demolished. On Saturday 6 September 1986 this platform is still in situ but looking decidedly unkempt and uncared for, as is the still open up platform and its building, as Class 101 three-car DMU set No B823 restarts from the stop as the 1635 Severn Beach-Bristol Temple Meads service. The appearance of the station is not one to inspire confidence and a feeling of safety!

With nature reclaiming the down platform and the up building now in private hands, as an upholstery business, the ambience is much improved. The entrance is now at the far end of the building, past the South Road residents' garages, seen on the left. Although surrounded by parkland and having a decent residential air, First Great Western's new 'Help Point' was stolen within days of installation in February 2010! Traffic flows have nearly doubled during the first decade of the 21st century, helped by a regular service pattern. On 3 September 2010 No 143620 begins the final stretch of its run as the 1154 Severn Beach-Bristol Temple Meads service. *Mike Mensing/MJS*

MONTPELIER was opened with the line on 1 October 1874, and was the first stop on the route from Bristol to Severn Beach after leaving the main line at Narroways Junction. As with Redland, there were originally two platforms as well as access to a coal yard from the down line, by way of a bridge across Station Road; this closed in 1966. The up platform once boasted graceful and magnificent buildings on either side of the footbridge, but these disappeared after the singling of the route. On Saturday 11 May 1985 unit No B126, formed of coach W55026, leaves as the 1540 Severn Beach-Bristol Temple Meads working.

Apart from a more modern DMU type, relatively little has changed by 3 September 2010, apart from tree growth, a drain on the platform, the support to the down steps from the footbridge now being of metal rather than the previous stone, and the appearance of graffiti on both sides of the running line. A young lady waits to board the 1203 Bristol Temple Meads-Avonmouth local operated by No 143611 for her short trip to Clifton Down. With the cascading following the introduction of new rolling stock elsewhere in the UK, 2011 should see the introduction of Class 150/1s onto the route, which will provide an extra 30 seats per train. *Mike Mensing/MJS*

MONTPELIER, being closer to the centre of Bristol, is a long-established area with buildings of character. More recently it has acquired a bohemian reputation, with many organic and vegetarian eateries, and it is the closest railway station to Gloucestershire County Cricket ground in Nevil Road. With 19 staff at the turn of the 20th century, it became unstaffed from 17 July 1967, but despite this the regular service of this century has seen patronage increase from around 60,000 in 2000 to more than 86,000 by 2009. Class 121 No W55026, seen on the previous page leaving for Bristol, is here arriving, with the 1445 service for Severn Beach, on Saturday 11 May 1985, having just passed through the 288-yard Montpelier Tunnel. *Mike Mensing*

Bristol Temple Meads (New) and engine sheds

BRISTOL TEMPLE MEADS: Oops! A derailment is unwelcome on the railway at any time, but at the throat of a very busy station it is especially irksome. Viewed from a departing train on 15 August 1959, a BR Standard Class 3 2-6-2T approaches the station and is about to pass a stricken No 9488 on the 233-yard Avon Viaduct over the Floating Harbour. Note the wood blocks supporting jacks, the lack of hi-vis vests, and cloth caps in places of helmets, in those halcyon pre-H&S days! There also does not appear to be a look-out to warn of approaching traffic!

A few moments earlier, the photographer's train takes water in the station platform. The fireman of No 7784 watches the bag, with his driver controlling the flow on the ground, as the fireman of No 8744 keeps his eye on the two young visitors. Note the gas lamp, the parcels trolley, water column, old-style station nameplate and the over-arching canopy – all long since gone. While the colour-light gantry might seem a modern innovation, it had been in place here since 1935. *Both Gerald Adams, MJS collection*

BRISTOL TEMPLE MEADS: The original Temple Meads terminus opened on 31 August 1840, to a design by Isambard Kingdom Brunel, as the western end of the GWR main line from Paddington. Such was its success, with a number of separate railway companies wishing to use it, that it soon became evident that further facilities were required. These finally came in the 1870s, with a through station being built to a design by Francis Fox, alongside but at a curving angle to the old terminus station. Initially with three new platforms, the site progressively developed and passenger facilities eventually expanded to 15 platforms served by eight running lines. On 28 September 1959 No 82043 stands with the empty stock of the 8.22am local from Witham and Yatton.

In the same position on 26 March 1982, No 33023 is also coupled to empty stock, but the view has changed with the cutting back of Culverhouse's 1936 canopy to accommodate the installation of the hideous mailbag conveyor system, which was abandoned from 1998.

On 4 September 2010 the monstrosity is still in situ, its drab exterior detracting from the otherwise magnificent overall design of the station. Note that a new, brick-built cabin has replaced the one from 1982, but it is still not a thing of beauty! No 143621 is temporarily empty stock, before it takes its turn to run to Weston-super-Mare.
Mike Mensing/John Acton, MJS collection/MJS

BRISTOL TEMPLE MEADS: The advent of diesels was not welcomed by steam enthusiasts, but at least the Western Region of BR maintained its individuality by introducing diesel-hydraulic locos, compared to the far more ubiquitous diesel-electrics. The 'Warship' Class is now, in hindsight, beloved of modern enthusiasts. On 21 September 1959 No D809 *Champion* – just one month old – has yet to be disfigured with a yellow front end as it enters the station with 'The Bristolian' express from London. Withdrawn in October 1971, it was cut up in Swindon Works one year later. The new order is also evidenced by the 'whiskered' DMU in the background.

Time marches on and some of the more than 8 million passengers that now use the station annually are seen on 4 September 2010, as 'Super Voyager' No 221140 arrives with the 0642 Newcastle-Penzance CrossCountry service – a much longer journey than endured by *Champion* above! To the left, No 150121 is the more modern DMU type as it waits to continue its journey as the 1042 Gloucester-Weymouth service. *Gerald Adams, MJS collection/MJS*

BRISTOL TEMPLE MEADS: Two more 'Warships', but slightly later and in transition: No D852 *Tenacious*, with the small yellow front end, stands in the middle road, while D813 *Diadem*, still with no yellow marking, leaves with 1A30 for Paddington in April 1962. D852 was one of 33 Class 43s built between 1960 and 1962 by the North British Locomotive Co, whereas D813, and D809 on the previous page, were Swindon products and classified as Class 42. The NBL locos had different power units and transmissions from their siblings and proved not to be as reliable as the Swindon products. However, these two were withdrawn within three months of each other – in October 1971 and January 1972.

The successor to the 'Warships' and the 'Westerns', swept away in a cull of hydraulics on front-line BR(W) workings, was to be the Class 50, cascaded from the WCML following the introduction of electrics on the route out of Euston. With a canopy again cut short by the emergence of the ugly mailbag conveyor housing, No 50001 *Dreadnought*, looking rather shabby in its corporate blue livery, waits to leave with an up express on 6 November 1982. New in December 1967 as D401, but without a name until April 1978, its end came from Laira depot on 19 April 1991. *John Chalcraft collection/MJS collection*

BRISTOL TEMPLE MEADS: When built in the 1870s expansion, the tracks underneath the impressive curving train shed handled all the main-line and through traffic. Initially there were six platform faces under cover, but four of these – effectively two island platforms – were removed in the 1930s, giving the layout we know today. At what was originally Platform 1, DMU set No B398 (formed of carriages 53632 and 51416) stands as the 1155 service to Severn Beach on 8 August 1991. An HST set departs for the north in the background.

On 4 September 2010 the layout is the same, with empty coaching stock again parked on the middle road, but two of the three information screens have been lost from the on-platform bracket; the now de rigueur yellow safety line has been applied; and the motive power is newer, with the crews about to change shifts. With anxious passengers thronging the new arrival, No 158798 is running some 15 minutes behind time as it comes to rest as the 1042 Southampton Central-Great Malvern cross country service. *Both MJS*

BRISTOL TEMPLE MEADS: The eastern end of the old Platform 1, now functioning as Platform 5, shows the delightful architectural style of the train shed screen and the canopy giving cover to waiting passengers. 'Patriot' No 45506 *The Royal Pioneer Corps*, complete with low-sided Stanier tender and 82E (Bristol Barrow Road) shed code on the smokebox, blows off as it stands in the station on 6 August 1960, after relieving the loco that had brought in the 'M232' special holiday working from Paignton to Leeds. No 44560 ... in the middle road with a rake of parcels vans.

Moving forward 50 years and one month, the need to change engines has long since disappeared, as also have loco-hauled long-distance trains. Units now rule the roost – which can give greater flexibility but also can be restrictive operationally – and on 4 September 2010 one of Mr Branson's former 'Voyagers' is now in CrossCountry hands. No 220010 – once named *Ribble Voyager* – has already come further and will travel further than the 'Patriot', the train being the 0825 Penzance-Glasgow Central through working. *John Edgington/MJS*

BRISTOL TEMPLE MEADS: We now concentrate on Platform 3, the old pre-1930s No 4 and, more recently, No 9! With the sharp curve of the tracks and train shed obvious from this angle, No 6391 waits patiently on 26 August 1956 for its queues of waiting passengers to board another holiday extra. 'Castle' No 5094 *Tretower Castle* blows off in the middle road as it waits with its own rake of carriages.

Now self-evidently Platform 3, it begins to accumulate a handful of early leavers from work at 4.00pm on 14 October 1971. 'Hymek' No D7038 casually trundles through on the middle line with its up freight. Note the installation of the cone-shaped lamps and evidence of parcels awaiting dispatch.

Nearly 30 years later the train shed survives in its magnificent glory and has also had a recent repaint. The decorative lamps have gone, as has the clock, but new signage is in place, both 'hard copy' and digital display, as an unidentified 'Super Voyager' draws to a halt at the end of its journey as the 1007 Manchester Piccadilly-Bristol CrossCountry duty on 4 September 2010. *Richard Casserley/Tom Heavyside/MJS*

BRISTOL TEMPLE MEADS: In the days when such things could happen, No 37086 backs a parcels van alongside bay Platform 2 at 6.08pm on Saturday 7 July 1979, having brought it attached to the 11.40am Newcastle-Paignton cross-country working. No 50042 *Triumph* will take the passenger train onwards to its destination. The driver watches carefully as he reverses without hitch but, sadly, he was not so fortunate as he pulled away from the bay, becoming derailed just past the platform end! No 08935 is on the right.

Locomotives are very much the rarity at Temple Meads today, apart from those hauling freight through the station, and there is precious little in the way of shunting needed with modern services and traffic flows. On 4 September 2010 No 150246 stands as empty stock in the platform, which, apart from the appearance of the yellow stripe and the absence of parcels trolleys, is little changed from 1979. The lineside trees have grown, the siding is now largely unused and the city's taller buildings can be seen in the distance, peering over the DMU. *Mike Mensing/MJS*

BRISTOL TEMPLE MEADS: We are now at the southern end of the station, with the panoramic view showing both the graceful curve of the 1870s train shed and the lower, more individual canopies from the 1930s. It does not seem so long ago, but this view of a loco-hauled passenger turn is approaching 30 years old. On 26 March 1982 No 47124 restarts the southern journey of the 0815 Birmingham New Street-Plymouth cross-country working. Released to traffic from Brush on 1 February 1964 as No D1714, it was to receive its TOPS number ten years later and to keep it until withdrawal, from Tinsley depot, on 5 June 1989. Scrapping came at MC Processors, Glasgow, in November 1990. Note the patched platform surface after the installation of the lighting.

At what is now designated Platform 10, No 159004, in South West Trains livery, forms the 1010 Southampton Central-Cardiff Central service on 4 September 2010. Lighting has again been changed, but the platform properly resurfaced on this occasion. The coaching stock underneath the train shed is for the next day's 'Torbay Express', which will be hauled by preserved No 6024 *King Edward I*, a new running-in board has been erected (foreground), and the whole retains the same (albeit temporary) peaceful atmosphere of the earlier picture. *John Acton, MJS collection/MJS*

BRISTOL TEMPLE MEADS: Immediately to the south of the station the many tracks are spanned by the large girder bridge taking the A4 road out of the city. Looking south on 21 July 1982, No 31239 approaches the station with a rake of vans working from Malago Vale Carriage Sidings to Old Oak Common. New from Brush as No D5666 in November 1960 and immediately going to work from March depot in East Anglia, this Type 2 diesel became No 31239 in March 1974, then 31439 on 6 April 1984. Named *North Yorkshire Moors Railway* on 19 September 1992 – the name since removed – it was one of the relatively few remaining in service at the time of writing. Note the iconic, though not architecturally stunning, multi-coloured housing in the distance.

The passage of 28 years has seen the prolific growth of trees both on the right and in the distance, softening the surroundings of the station, as No 143621 passes under the girder bridge and enters Platform 3 with the 1110 local service from Weston-super-Mare to Bristol Parkway. *Edwin Wilmshurst/MJS*

BRISTOL TEMPLE MEADS: The magic of steam and a lost era! Living and breathing, and openly displaying its latent power, No 5024 *Carew Castle* leaves with the southbound 'Devonian' on August Bank Holiday, 6 August 1956. The platform is peopled with enthusiasts, young and old, with many of them spotting at the head of the slope at the platform end. Note the preponderance of the more formal attire of the day, suits and/or jackets and trousers, and, as presumably it was not a particularly warm day despite the sunshine, the number of mackintoshes. Note also the proliferation of colour-light clusters, and the gentlemen strolling in the 'six-foot', with not a hi-vis vest in sight!. The steam in the background emanates from Bath Road shed.

By comparison, the same vista on 4 September 2010 is denuded. 'Super Voyager' No 221140 – named *Vasco da Gama* on 21 September 2002, but stripped of this honour exactly five years later – makes its exit from the station, but without the grandeur and pride of the 'Castle', forming the 0642 Newcastle-Penzance CrossCountry 'express'. Note the wilderness where Bath Road shed once stood. *Hugh Ballantyne/MJS*

BRISTOL TEMPLE MEADS: Another view from the south end, facing north and with a wider angle, shows the sheer scale of the real estate occupied by the railway. On 26 August 1956 'Hall' No 5971 *Merevale Hall* waits for its turn to leave with a train for the holiday haunts of Devon and Cornwall. To the left a '57xx' 0-6-0PT shunts in the middle road under the train shed, two tanks stand with their respective rakes in the then outer platforms on the right, and a further tank engine moves light towards the photographer. The water column rests idly until the next thirsty loco needs refreshment.

More than 50 years later the station is basically as before, but with operational needs, traffic flows and changes in thinking dictating alterations. New lighting again graces the refurbished platform, as No 150265 is once more in motion, after pausing halfway through its 1100 Cardiff Central-Taunton roster. Usage of platforms has changed over time and, more recently, the two 'isolated' platform faces on the right have been brought back from parcels to passenger use. The normal Paddington-Bristol HSTs now use these platforms rather than drawing into the main station. Note the rationalisation of the track in that sector compared with the earlier picture. *Mike Mensing/MJS*

BRISTOL TEMPLE MEADS: Moving away from the confines of the station, we now view it from the vantage point of the girder bridge carrying the A4. On 9 October 1965 No 82044 chuffs its merry way out of the station with a four-coach empty stock movement to Malago Vale. This autumn day seems dull and misty, with only the steam working to enliven things. Steam was due to cease on the Western Region by the end of 1965, but sadly the 'Standard 3' will not even make that deadline, being withdrawn from Bath Green Park shed the month after this view.

Fifteen years of progress sees the station basically as before, with just the 'musical chairs' of colour-lights the most noticeable feature, but beyond the skyline is changing. We are deep into the diesel loco-hauled era, with the Class 50s arriving and running alongside 45s/46s and 47s, and there has been much rationalisation of trackwork in the foreground, between the running lines and the Bath Road shed boundary. A not uncommon sight on holiday trains in this period, double-headed Nos 31262 and 31133 gather speed as they regain the road with the 1235 Birmingham New Street-Paignton service on Saturday 26 July 1980. They need to hurry, as No 46008, adjacent, is waiting to follow with the 1040 service from Manchester Piccadilly to the same destination.

The cityscape is again in flux, with new buildings apparent, while on the ground the track is as before, although the sidings to the left are largely now unused. Ringing the changes in motive power, an example of the new era of freight motive power, No 66139, in its rather garish EWS livery, passes through the main train shed with 6H67, the 0751 Cardiff Tidal-Tavistock Junction empty stock on 24 September 2003. *Tom Heavyside/Mike Mensing/Mike Goodfield*

BRISTOL BATH ROAD SHED: Railway ants! Depot Open Days have long held a fascination for enthusiasts, and on 23 October 1965 all ages and both sexes enjoy the fine weather at Bath Road shed and the opportunity to view, 'cab' – and climb on! – a variety of steam locos that are fast disappearing. The undoubted focus of attention is No 7029 *Clun Castle*, but 'Teddy Bear' No D9517 and a variety of tanks, including No 6141 and 'Jinty' No 47276, also receive their share of homage. In the background, the shed has Classes 47 and 45 as well as 'Hymeks' and 'Warships', and on the right the 'Blue Pullman' set. One wonders what apoplexy today's Health & Safety officers would have at the mountaineering escapades on the locomotives!

Another showcase event in the same year features Stanier 'Black 5' No 44856 with a full load of coal in its tender. By the time of this view it was a servant of ex-GWR Oxley (Wolverhampton) shed, but had previously been the preserve of ex-LMS depots. At Leeds Holbeck for many years, it moved south to Derby in August 1953, followed by Saltley, Nottingham and Saltley again before transfer within the West Midlands to Oxley. Withdrawal came on 25 February 1967. Sadly, despite its excellent appearance here, it was not spared the cutter's torch. *Ben Ashworth/MJS collection*

BRISTOL BATH ROAD SHED: The design and layout has changed over the years since the first shed was opened on the Bath Road site in 1850. A six-road stone-built affair, it was extended in 1859 and had a separate building added in 1877, but the demands on it continued unabated, resulting in demolition from 1933, with a new 10-road brick-built replacement erected adjacent to the Bath Road retaining wall in 1934. That new shed can be seen in the right background a couple of years later, as No 3433 pauses for its portrait as it prepares to leave the yard for its next duty.

The steam shed was an early casualty of the introduction of diesels, closing to the old traction on 12 September 1960. The shed was then itself demolished and a purpose-built diesel facility put in its place. As can be seen from this view of No 31144 on shed on 6 August 1988, much infrastructure has been added, not least the tall lighting towers. New from Brush on 5 November 1959 as D5562, it spent its early years in East Anglia, mostly at Norwich, before migrating north to Immingham depot in May 1968. Its working life ended at Springs Branch (Wigan) depot in January 1996. *Both MJS collection*

BRISTOL BATH ROAD SHED: A spotter's delight: back in the halcyon days of steam the scene, viewed from Temple Meads station on 9 July 1960, looks the epitome of the 'permanent way', but there remained just two months for steam to rule the roost! With south Bristol stretching out in the distance at 4.00pm on this bright, sunny day, No 5090 *Neath Abbey* stands on the left with sister loco No 5078 *Beaufort* to the right, bearing the 'M56' reporting code. Others present include 'Standard 3' tanks, a 'Mogul' and two 0-6-0PTs.

Forward a decade, and part of the first incarnation of the diesel depot is behind No D7047 on 14 October 1971. At this time the tenure of the diesel-hydraulics on the Western Region was becoming less secure and this 'Hymek' lasted just three months beyond the date of this view, to be cut up in Swindon Works eight months after that in August 1972. The vast majority of 'Warships' had also been taken from squadron service, and no doubt the rather forlorn-looking pair in the background are among these. Alongside them is the 'Western Pullman', Class 25 and 31 locomotives, and another 'Hymek'. *Hugh Ballantyne/Tom Heavyside*

BRISTOL BATH ROAD SHED: At 0711 on 21 May 1995, the early-morning spring sunshine adds an attractive light to this zoom shot from Temple Meads station, showing six roads of the shed closest to the offices, with, from left to right, Nos 47841, 47739, 47746 and 47539. More 47s shelter inside, and it is obvious which is the motive power of choice here! Note the InterCity livery applied to the depot's front, echoing that on many of the locomotives, and Holy Nativity church on the Wells Road in the background.

How are the mighty fallen, and what a difference two years can make! What was once the largest depot in the area now presents a mournful and forlorn spectacle on 13 June 1997, with no sign of life and obviously abandoned with an uncertain future. Rumours were rife of it merely being mothballed, with possible future use as a centre for commissioning the new Class 66s, but already there would need to be much work to reinstate it to something even approaching its former glory.

The final curtain. Demolished despite many grandiose schemes for the site, including sports facilities, shops and housing, all faded into apathy, inertia and funding problems, and now the site lays waste. The view on 4 September 2010 is not a happy one, and not one to lift passing travellers' spirits! *All MJS*

BRISTOL BATH ROAD SHED: A last look at slightly happier times on 16 March 1958, with 2-6-2T No 5574 standing on shed between duties of clearing the piles of discarded ash and clinker, during its very short four-month stay at Bath Road in the spring and early summer of 1958. Built in 1929, it was a well-travelled loco, serving, during its BR tenure, Gloucester Horton Road, Tondu, Aberbeeg, Cardiff Cathays, Bristol, and back to Tondu, from where the end came on 29 November of that year.

By 21 May 1995 the more menial loco tasks on shed were undertaken for the most part by Class 08 shunters. No 08668 stands at the head of a rake of Class 47s of many colours. Right to left, they are Nos 47509, 47432, 47527 and 47508, with south Bristol in the background and the main shed to the right. All are withdrawn, from as far back as 1992 and, for 47508, 1993.

By comparison, the much healthier-looking class members, in RES livery, standing outside the main shed are in rude health, but the shed is not, seen only a matter of days before closure. Left to right, the locomotives are Nos 47789, 47727, 47739, 47746 and 47539, which would all serve into the 21st century. *Gerald Adams, MJS collection/MJS (2)*

BRISTOL BATH ROAD SHED: This rare view of the rear of the depot, on 5 June 1987, shows the turntable being used for practical road use, as there is little space for the articulated lorry to turn round otherwise! The station avoiding line from North Somerset Junction, by way of St Philips Marsh, is glimpsed in the bottom right, crossing the girder bridge over the River Avon. *Mike Mensing*

BRISTOL ST PHILIP'S MARSH SHED: Not the most attractive of names, but in steam days it was certainly an attractive proposition for any enthusiast. Next to the shed in November 1962 9F 2-10-0 No 92246 waits to work back to its home depot of Cardiff Canton, after working in with a freight from South Wales. An unidentified 'Hall' stands behind. New in February 1958, the 9F's initial allocation was to Old Oak Common, on the outskirts of London, but South Wales beckoned in November 1960. There were then various changes of home before removal from active stock at Gloucester Horton Road shed on 15 January 1966, when it was less than eight years old! *John Chalcraft*

BRISTOL ST PHILIP'S MARSH SHED: Another long-distance visitor, Western Region 'Hall' 4-6-0 No 5976 *Ashwicke Hall* of Exeter shed, stands on the coal road by the coaling stage ramp in July 1956. The use of a ramp to lift coal supplies was a common device employed by the GWR, and a surviving example is to be found at the Great Western Society site at Didcot. Renumbered to 3951 when converted to oil in the late 1940s, the locomotive reverted to 5976 on 30 November 1948 and served at Exeter until January 1959. The next 5½ years saw it serve out time in South Wales after a brief stint at Old Oak Common between leaving Devon and 14 July 1962. The end was on 20 July 1964 at Pontypool Road shed.

The steam shed at St Philip's Marsh was opened in July 1910 and closed on 17 June 1964. Thereafter the site of the main shed was demolished and the section to the west of Victoria Road abandoned to non-railway development. That road is on a lower level beyond the bushes and there is just one small part of the coaling ramp left in situ, glimpsed beyond the buffer stop on 2 September 2010. This part of the old yard has been totally redefined with the development of the new diesel depot.*John Chalcraft Collection/MJS*

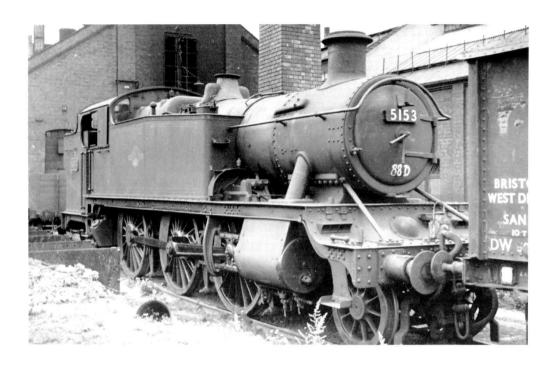

BRISTOL ST PHILIP'S MARSH SHED: In a siding by the shed wall on an unidentified date, 2-6-2T No 5153 seems to be a long way from home, judging by its painted 88D (Merthyr Tydfil) 'shedplate', but its records show that it was never allocated to South Wales during its BR history! Withdrawn in November 1964, this could well be around that time, as it is sandwiched between a Sand van and a wooden coal wagon and, therefore, unlikely to be in active service or to return to its parent shed at Leamington.

As there is no possibility of a comparative view, we take the opportunity of demonstrating the development on what was the site of the shed building. The far building marks roughly the length of the old shed, but its width reached as far as the fencing. Nowadays, this is Bristol's fruit market, seen from the remaining railway section at this western end of the current layout at St Philip's Marsh. *MJS collection/MJS*

BRISTOL ST PHILIP'S MARSH SHED: Like a time capsule – and how we might wish we could be in one to revisit such views. On 16 March 1958 the inside of the shed's roundhouse sees, from left to right, an ex-LMS Stanier 8F and Nos 8491, 46517, 3773 (with another '84xx' in steam beyond) and 5315. All were to remain in action for at least another four years, with the exception of No 5315, which succumbed to the inevitable in January 1959. Note the wooden covering for the turntable pit, a slightly unusual precaution, as most pits were left open.

Outside in the yard two years earlier, the new order has arrived. Without any of the yellow and black warning stripes that were to come, and not yet having lost its original identity, No 13187 was still a youngster on 18 March 1956, being new from Derby Works the previous November. Looking spruce with its 'cycling lion' BR logo proudly displayed, it was renumbered D3187 in June 1961, then 08120 under TOPS in February 1974, before losing the battle at Darlington in October 1981. Before ending up in the North East it had served BR(W) for just short of 12 years before transferring to BR(M) on 16 September 1967. *Both Gerald Adams, MJS collection*

BRISTOL ST PHILIP'S MARSH SHED: A common sight on the ex-GWR lines in steam days was that company's ubiquitous 0-6-0PTs. On 18 March 1956 a selection stand in line waiting their next call; No 9729 is at the head, with three more and two '84xx' types behind. Presumably this was a Sunday, as the locos are not in steam and they would no doubt be out working if it were a weekday. A Bristol engine for much of its life, the end for No 9729 came at Exeter on 22 November 1964, just 12 months after it left the Avon. It was scrapped at Cashmore's, Newport, in March 1965.

The redesign of the depot following closure of the steam shed has meant that an exact comparative view is impossible, but this is a general view of the current yard looking in the same direction as above. On 2 September 2010 the side of the new shed built for the Class 180 'Adelantes' leads our eye to a selection of infrastructure machines made redundant by the failure of Jarvis, with depot 08 No 08663 alongside, complete with the regulation 'zebra stripes'. *Gerald Adams, MJS collection/MJS*

BRISTOL ST PHILIP'S MARSH SHED: Having seen inside the steam shed, we now peer into the diesel equivalent on 14 March 1999 and see two HST sets, with power cars Nos 43030 (left) and 43149 (right) in their smart green and grey GW livery of the time. The former was to be named *Christian Lewis Trust* in July of the following year, while No 43149 already wears a *BBC Wales Today* plate. Note the suspended blanket at the end of the row with the arched cut-out.

A little over 11 years later, the blanket has gone, replaced by more solid constructions. Inside on 2 September 2010 DMU units Nos 150234 and 143621 are in for servicing before returning to front-line duties. The pits have seen little alteration over the years and the snaking pipes are common to both views. The lighting looks the same, but the roof lights seem to have been turned through a 90-degree angle. *Both MJS*

Dr Day's Junction to Hallen Marsh Junction

DR DAY'S JUNCTION: Half a mile north-east of Temple Meads, Dr Day's Junction is the northern apex of a triangular arrangement that provides direct access from the south and east for trains to run north and avoid the centre of Bristol. In this view of No 92213 on 12 October 1965, the 9F is rounding Bristol Loop – opened on 29 May 1886 – before continuing its journey north with the rake of box vans. The layout here has seen a swap over the years, with the Loop initially being quadruple and the right-hand line double. The four-track layout on the right, leading to Temple Meads, came into use in January 1933, after the demolition of a signal box that formerly stood between the loco and the small shed in the centre of the picture.

Moving a few yards to the right, the Loop is seen in wider angle, at precisely 1622 on 5 August 1987, as No 47122 eases round the curve with a northbound Speedlink freight service. The surviving line from the 1965 reduction of tracks on the Loop, seen opposite, has now disappeared, leaving just the two plain lines, and there has been much new construction over the intervening 18 years. Initially set up in 1983, to provide fast and varied air-braked freight services, Speedlink was hit by a number of factors during the decade, leading to its demise in 1991.

Now looking towards Temple Meads on the same day, the main route to the north is busy, with Class 108 DMU set No B964, forming the 1444 Severn Beach-Temple Meads local, moving away from the camera. The driver of the Class 33 is using the lineside telephone to clear the way for what is presumed to be a late-running 1210 Portsmouth Harbour-Cardiff train, and in the centre a Class 47 heads another Speedlink service towards the photographer. The old GWR water tower is still in place in the middle distance. The nearside double lines were removed in 1970, but such has been the explosion in traffic over the past 15 years that in 2010 Network Rail was planning to reinstate them! *MJS/Mike Mensing (2)*

LAWRENCE HILL: A gloriously captured view from the remains of the old MR line from Fishponds to the original Temple Meads on 12 July 1979 sees No 31159 heading north with an engineer's spoil train, bound for Filton tip. The main lines to the 'new' Temple Meads are on the left but have no connection with the platform lines here. They were taken out of use in 1984, around the same time as the goods yard on the right was abandoned. The curve on the extreme right was opened in February 1970, to give access to Avonside Wharf. The cement terminal in the centre of the picture remained until the mid-1990s, being worked on this date by No 03382, seen stabled under the shed awning immediately behind the '31'.

Moving further to the right across the old railway bridge, on the late afternoon of 6 April 1988 the goods yard is empty apart from the cement materials, as No 47079, in its two-tone-grey Railfreight Construction livery, slowly reverses its 'Avon Refuse Train' towards the Barrow Road Waste Depot. Note that the gas holder in the distance, seen in the earlier picture, has been removed. *John Chalcraft , John Chalcraft/Mike Mensing*

LAWRENCE HILL: On the up relief line platform in the early 1960s, all is momentarily quiet on this slightly misty day, with the signalman seated by his window and presumably not expecting a call in the immediate future. Ancient gas lamp standards adorn the platforms, a covered footbridge connects the two platforms, and large canopies are in place to provide shelter on all four platform faces. The 38-lever signal box survived for 80 years until 1970.

Fifty years later the scene is very different. All evidence of the former main lines is hidden by trees and bushes; the site of the signal box is now protected by metal fencing, forbidding access to this end of the platform; the station buildings have disappeared, with a very rudimentary one at the far end of the down platform; there is no longer a station footbridge, access now being via the main road beyond; lighting is now only at the far end; the yard to the right is still handling goods, but now only by road; and tower blocks have sprung up to peer down on the station. *N. C. Simmons, Hugh Davies collection/MJS*

LAWRENCE HILL: We now have a view of the main lines, albeit in the last years of their use. At precisely 1154 on 26 November 1983, just months before the lines were closed and lifted, No 47256 rumbles south with a rake of empty four-wheeled stone wagons. Note that the erstwhile platforms on both sides of these lines have been stripped back. New as No D1934 from Brush in March 1966 and going first to Bristol Bath Road shed, it became No 47256 in February 1974, under TOPS, and remained one of the very few of its immediate sisters not to be renumbered thereafter. Withdrawal was from Immingham depot on 28 January

With the removal of the former footbridge, a comparative view is perforce from the current access to the platform from the nearby roadway. With gloom very evident in the 1983 portrait, the vista on 4 September 2010 presents a much more pleasant scene, despite the absence of tracks. The greenery softens the bare aspect and shields the industrial scene to the right. The small waiting shelter, with its new lighting, is also accompanied by a new Help Point, recently installed by FGW. Happily, there are plans for the empty trackbed to once more receive trains. *Mike Mensing/MJS*

LAWRENCE HILL: Seen from the station footbridge on 26 November 1983, the up relief line platform is occupied by Class 118 three-car DMU set No B436, operating the 1140 Bristol Temple Meads-Severn Beach local service. With its exhaust betraying its restart, it moves past the remains of the station buildings and goods yard. Note that the far end of both platforms are now out of normal use. The old MR railway bridge is in the distance.

Despite the absence of the tracks on the right, the view on 4 September 2010 is still more attractive that that above. The train is yet another for Severn Beach – the 1116 from Temple Meads – but now with just two cars in the form of unit No 143618. The waiting shelters may be basic but they are not unattractive, and even the factory unit is clean and purposeful. On the nearside platform, a mother waits to take her child to Weymouth. *Mike Mensing/MJS*

LAWRENCE HILL: Originally part of the Bristol & South Wales Union Railway, operating between Temple Meads and New Passage for the ferry to South Wales, Lawrence Hill station was opened on 8 September 1863. That first route is to the right, with what became the main lines to the left, in this view looking south towards Temple Meads, a mile away. Viewed from the road bridge, No 45041 *Royal Tank Regiment* is about to pass non-stop through the station with the 1028 Taunton-Birmingham New Street service of Saturday 5 May 1979. Although the trackwork is clean, the railway's boundary on the right certainly needs some TLC!

By 4 September 2010 the open view to the right has been lost, as has the old housing on the left and the left-hand track. Since the latter was removed in the mid-1980s, there have been calls for some sort of replacement, and in 2010 the latest thinking is to reinstate the former two roads. Note that, beyond the bridge, one of the tracks has been retained, to add operational flexibility into Bristol. *Mike Mensing/MJS*

LAWRENCE HILL: Our final look at the station is on Saturday 6 August 1983, as single-car Class 121 No B126, coach No W55026, in BR's blue and grey corporate livery, is sufficient for the traffic anticipated on the 1223 Severn Beach-Bristol Temple Meads stopping service. With youngsters at the top of the stairs watching the train leave, it is quite possible that the more elderly couple are the only passengers to have alighted.

Another Saturday – 4 September 2010 – sees little disturbance beyond the railway, with just chimneys lost from the building above the train, but at platform level the provision and ambience are much changed. The comparative service, the 1035 from Avonmouth to Temple Meads, is now formed of the two carriages of unit No 143618; there is now a small shelter; a short fence has been erected to dissuade would-be trespassers; new lighting has been erected; and a new Help Point installed. Though not dramatic, passenger numbers have steadily grown, to reach around **70,000** per year. *Mike Mensing/MJS*

STAPLETON ROAD, together with Lawrence Hill, opened on 8 September 1863 but, unlike its neighbour, it was to gain added importance when it became a junction station in 1874, with the opening of the branch to Clifton Down. Trains to and from Cardiff also used the station for a period, but this had ceased by the date of this view. On Saturday 14 February 1981 Class 101 three-car DMU set No B810 passes through non-stop with the 1530 Bristol Temple Meads-Cardiff Central duty. Note the large Bristol Co-op Laundry building in the background, amid the multitude of terraced housing.

Happily, there are once more occasional Cardiff trains stopping here, but the more local services are augmented by stops on the Gloucester-Westbury axis. The present-day view lacks the former main-line tracks, the course of which has been left to nature, and the platform limits have been reinforced by steel fencing. On 4 September 2010 No 143612 slows for the stop as the 1034 Bristol Temple Meads-Avonmouth local service. The colour-light signal post is still in situ, but with a more modern light fixture and safety caging for the step ladder. *Mike Mensing/MJS*

STAPLETON ROAD was once a very busy station, with the only Bristol stops between South Wales and the South Coast being made here. The four platforms (from 1888) were furnished with large canopies and even a refreshment room on the island platform. All were joined by a covered footbridge, but those halcyon days have gone as another single car, Class 121 No B133, coach No 55033, draws to a halt while working the 12.22 Severn Beach-Bristol Temple Meads stopper on 29 October 1980, underneath the now coverless footbridge. In the right distance, the large girder bridge crossing a road and the River Frome carried the main-line tracks until the mid-1980s.

Although self-evidently the same place, it is oh so different on the right-hand side. No 150249 speeds through the station non-stop as the 1000 Cardiff Central-Taunton service on Saturday 4 September 2010. The truncated footbridge has protection to prevent the unwary from stepping into thin air, as the former main-line platforms and trackbed have been adopted by 'Eastside Roots', a community eco-garden centre. One wonders what they will do if the tracks are reinstated! *John Chalcraft/MJS*

STAPLETON ROAD: Here is another view of a train entering from the south, this time taken from the footbridge. With housing nestling close by the railway boundary, No 47232 climbs away from the centre of Bristol during the early evening of 10 August 1979, as the late-running 1356 Penzance-Birmingham New Street express. The city's inexorable sprawl northwards and its insatiable appetite for land for building is clear from this view.

The cityscape has not altered, even the tall telegraph pole still at its crazy angle and the skyscrapers on the skyline, but the growth of trees has done much to soften any previous harshness. On 4 September 2010 No 150248 has a relatively short journey, operating as the 1010 service from Weston-super-Mare to Bristol Parkway, as it runs into the station. Note again the obsession with fencing to discourage further passage along the platforms. *Mike Mensing/MJS*

STAPLETON ROAD: Now looking north, the dilapidated condition of the station is no encouragement to patronage and one wonders whether the young lad on the up platform is spotting or loitering with intent! The large girder bridge is again seen in the background, together with the gas holder adjacent to Narroways Junction, as No W55033 arrives forming the 1856 Severn Beach-Bristol Temple Meads service. Serried rows of housing pepper the distant hillside.

The value of small, suburban stations can often be overlooked, but they can provide a convenient lifeline for their communities. On Saturday 4 September 2010 morning shoppers prepare to board the 1035 Avonmouth-Bristol Temple Meads service, ready for their trip to the city. The unsightly, derelict buildings have been swept aside, with yet more rudimentary shelters provided but offering precious little protection! The distant view is now camouflaged with greenery, virtually swamping the girder bridge. The left-hand wall, however, lifts the mood with a long mural by local artist Bill Guilding, which features characters illustrating local and historical themes. *Mike Mensing/MJS*

NARROWAYS JUNCTION is seen from a local footbridge, looking south towards Bristol. In the early 1960s an unidentified 'Castle' 4-6-0 hurries towards the city with a down express, probably bound for the West Country. The gas holder on the left has its own siding, occupied by coal wagons and accessed from both this main line and the MR route, out of sight to the left of the holder. Stapleton Road station is in the distance, with its own siding to the right at a lower level, and the branch to Avonmouth and beyond swings to the right. The semaphore signals vie for space!

By 13 June 1988 the gas holder remains but its siding has gone, as have the industrial structures around it. The main lines have recently been lifted, the Stapleton Road sidings have gone (closed in November 1965), and the branch to Avonmouth has been singled since 19 October 1970. Twin-car unit No 155309 handles the cross-country 1210 Portsmouth Harbour-Cardiff Central service. New in November 1987, this unit was short-lived in this guise, being split to form Nos 153309 and 153359 in September 1991.

Fifteen years later relatively little has changed apart from nature attempting reclamation in places. On 4 April 2003 Freightliner-liveried No 66506 hurries north with the 1541 Portbury-Mossend car transporter service. *Colour-Rail.com/Mike Mensing/Mike Goodfield*

ASHLEY HILL: Roughly midway between Stapleton Road and Ashley Hill station, the MR route from Fishponds to Clifton Down crossed the north-south GWR lines. It suffered bomb damage during the Second World War and was closed on 14 June 1965. The supporting abutments of the bridge carrying this line are clearly in view on 6 May 1969 as No D7012 drifts downhill from Ashley Hill station, in the upper left corner, with a rake of box vans as working '8B15'. These 'main-line' tracks were removed from 20 February 1984.

With security fencing and the growth of bushes and trees, the precise comparative location is now unattainable, so this view is from the footbridge a few yards further south. On 11 September 2010 the eastern abutment is still visible, now adorned with graffiti, as No 143620 descends along the erstwhile relief line as the 1215 local from Filton Abbey Wood to Weston-super-Mare, truncated at its northern end due to the closure of Bristol Parkway by an engineering possession. Note the appearance of new housing, visible despite the tree growth. *Hugh Ballantyne/MJS*

ASHLEY HILL: Approximately 2½ miles from Temple Meads, this station was a later addition to the initial line to New Passage, not opening until 13 August 1864, with just a single platform face. Doubling came in 1886, to be followed by the quadrupling of the running lines in April 1933. Those can be seen on 29 May 1959 in this delightful portrait of the up 'Bristolian' rushing through the station behind No 5085 *Evesham Abbey*, passing a down freight. Serving the residential area of Ashley Down, to the right of the view, the ... closed to local services on 23 November 1964 and the two tracks occupied here were, as seen before, removed 20 years later.

With the station and, indeed, the footbridge from which the above view was taken no more, the present-day aspect is from ground level. Once again, nature is working hard to reclaim lost ground, both at the lineside and on the old trackbed, as No 150127, internally renewed following transfer to FGW but still wearing the ex-Silverlink livery, heads for the city on an unidentified working, due to the weekend possession and blockade of Bristol Parkway, on 11 September 2010. *MJS collection/MJS*

FILTON: The area to the north-east of Bristol city centre has been populated by tall electricity pylons for many years. Part of the system is seen overlooking the line during the late afternoon of 3 April 1989 as 'old and new' meet, just to the north of Stallyfarm bridge and adjacent to the line to the Filton coal centre on the left. No 37066 heads north with a mixed rake of containers and, behind them, oil tanks, while No 156440 travels in the opposite direction with the 1536 Cardiff Central-Portsmouth Harbour service. The Class 156 unit is standing in for the recently introduced 155s, as these had been giving trouble.

The vantage point is the same, but the lens has zoomed in slightly to catch sight of Filton Abbey Wood station, the third facility to have graced Filton over the years. On 11 September 2010 No 158951 restarts from the station stop with the 1230 Cardiff Central-Portsmouth Harbour cross-country working. Opened on 11 March 1996, replacing the Junction station a hundred yards or so to the north, and initially as a two-platform affair, the third platform face was added in 2004, to overcome some of the bottleneck conditions caused by the myriad of traffic flows through the site. Note how the backdrop has changed dramatically with the growth of trees over the years. *Mike Mensing/MJS*

FILTON ABBEY WOOD: After opening in 1996, the station has grown in popularity, not just with the employees of the nearby MoD Procurement Division office complex, for whom it was largely engineered, but with many locals and commuters. Such was the success locally and the growth of through traffic that the narrow two-platform arrangement became increasingly restrictive. With some 'blue sky thinking', a railway employee devised the idea of a third platform face on the western (up) side, dedicated to the traffic to Cardiff and South Wales. This view from 4 March 2004 shows the original layout and preparatory work under way; the brick wall was to disappear.

The work was completed in impressively quick time, and this is the view on 28 June 2004, with the new platform open for business as No 150240 pulls in with the 1020 Bristol Temple Meads-Cardiff Central service. Note that, to the left, the electricity wires have gone underground, with the removal of at least one pylon, and that Nuttall, the contractors, have their logo displayed at the far end of the platform. The station has since become one of the busiest unstaffed facilities in the UK! *Both MJS*

FILTON ABBEY WOOD: Turning through 180 degrees to look north from the station footbridge, work is about to start and substantial changes are planned. On 4 March 2004 No 158871, in Alphaline grey livery, leaves the station with yet another Portsmouth Harbour-Cardiff Central working and prepares to run through the closed Junction station. Note the footpath to the limited car parking, with its dividing white line.

On 12 June 2004 track panels are in place for the new turnouts, the new line is in place, a new footpath climbs on the left, where it will meet the extended footbridge, and the original access path is buried under the panels. Virgin 'Voyager' No 220030 *Devon*

Voyager speeds past the work as 1E32, the 1158 Bristol Temple Meads-Newcastle CrossCountry roster.

The hot mid-summer sunshine beats down on No 67017 *Arrow* as it heads away from the Filton Abbey Wood stop at the rear of the 1247 Paignton-Cardiff Central service on 24 June 2010; No 67016 is at the head. The site is becoming naturalised, with the new footpath and area between the tracks now looking part of the scenery; and the new arrangement is working well. Notice how the stripe from the old footpath still shines forth! *All MJS*

FILTON ABBEY WOOD: To celebrate the satisfactory completion of the project, it was decided to name No 150243 *The Filton Partnership*, recognising the contributions made by the various parties. Having brought the guests to Filton as the 1144 special working from Bristol Temple Meads, the local Mayor and stakeholders John Hayes, Alan Wilson and David Smith pose for their portrait, complete with replica nameplate, smiling after a cloudburst!

The new line is open and all is neat and tidy. Carefully studying your photographer, the driver of 2B68, the 0920 Bristol Temple Meads-Cardiff Central local service, accelerates from the Abbey Wood stop and approaches the erstwhile Junction station (behind the camera) on 28 June 2004. *Both MJS*

FILTON JUNCTION: Opened in 1903 as plain 'Filton', what became the 'Junction' station (from 1 May 1910) replaced an earlier, single-platform facility to the south of the Filton-Frenchay road (later the A4174). When it opened, Filton was a small village, with a population of around 500, but such was the population explosion in this part of Bristol that this figure had risen to well over 12,000 by the 1960s! In this view looking south on 9 May 1964 we can glimpse the 5-ton crane standing in the goods yard, as well as the 78-lever signal box and the multi-crossed four-track layout. These three features disappeared from, respectively, late 1995, February 1971 and February 1984. Industrial units now stand on the goods yard site. Note the tall semaphores and the open aspect in the left distance.

Hardly recognisable as the same place, the replacement milepost still retains the 'three-quarters' marking. As with so much of our railway system, this view from 11 September 2010 is yet more evidence of just how much is swept away by time and 'progress'. *P. J. Garland, Roger Carpenter collection/MJS*

FILTON JUNCTION: Turning round to look north, the station is seen in all its glory on the same day as the previous 'past' photograph, 9 May 1964. A little over 60 years old, it still looks in fine shape, with track, platforms and buildings well cared for, although the paintwork on the buildings could do with some refreshing! At the outbreak of the Second World War the station employed 24 staff. From left to right, the lines served Avonmouth (diverging at the end of the platform); Patchway, Pilning and the Severn Tunnel (straight ahead); and Bristol Parkway, the north and London Paddington (right-hand platforms).

Only a little over a decade from closure, apart from the platforms still in situ nothing remains of the original station buildings. While Abbey Wood has undoubtedly been a success story, it is sad that such a magnificent edifice should have been summarily swept away. *P. J. Garland, Roger Carpenter collection/MJS*

FILTON JUNCTION: Standing on the eastern, 'London', side of the station and looking south, we have another view of 'The Bristolian', the 4.30pm Temple Meads-Paddington express, this time hauled by No 7019 *Fowey Castle*. Looking across to the relatively new housing in Filton in the late-1950s, the 78-lever signal box is seen again, in the background. One of the later 'Castles' built, No 7019 was new in May 1949 and allocated to Bristol Bath Road shed. Its stay there was 12 years before it travelled north to Wolverhampton Stafford Road in May 1961 and thence to nearby Oxley in September 1963. Withdrawal came from that shed in February 1965, less than 16 years after construction. *MJS collection*

FILTON JUNCTION: As the evening begins to draw in, No 47185 emits a slight plume of exhaust as it enters the station with a short five-van parcels train from South Wales, presumably bound for Temple Meads, at 2018 on Saturday 6 August 1983. The station is still open but, at this northern end, it has a spartan feel. New from Brush in October 1964 as No D1780, subsequent renumberings were to 47602 three months after this view, then 47824 in April 1989 and 47782 in February 1994. Named *Glorious Devon* at Exeter St David's station on 7 August 1985, the name was removed in February 1993, and the loco was withdrawn, from Old Oak Common depot, in September 2003.

Running late, partly due to the disruption from the engineering possession at Bristol Parkway, No 66589 speeds through the closed station on Saturday 11 September 2010 with 4O51, the 1000 Wentloog (Cardiff)-Southampton freightliner service. Note the siting of the colour-light at the end of the platform, and that the latter has had a length of its coping stones removed. Elsewhere, the greenery has again softened the surroundings. *Mike Mensing/MJS*

FISHPOOL: When constructed in 1910, the Avonmouth & Filton Railway was a single line joining the two places in rural surroundings on the northern edge of Bristol. It was to receive a boost from both World Wars, with Filton Airfield being constructed along part of its northern edge and, later, the establishment of the Bristol Aeroplane Company's works close by. Track-doubling took place in 1917 but, following withdrawal of passenger services in November 1964, the route reverted to single line in May 1966. At lunchtime on 3 October 1989 No 37059 *Port of Tilbury* is not unduly taxed with just two cargowaggons and three four-wheeled oil tanks as it is about to pass under Fishpool Hill bridge.

With the advent of increased coal imports to Avonmouth, the line was again doubled in 1994 and this came in very handy when the rebuilding of Filton Abbey Wood led to closure for a period and diversions were needed. Making good use of the line, the very smartly turned-out Virgin-liveried No 220020 *Wessex Voyager* heads 1E32, the 0725 Penzance-Newcastle CrossCountry express in the warm early summer sunshine of 24 June 2004. In recent times the vantage point has become known as 'dog mess alley'! *Mike Mensing/MJS*

FILTON WEST: With the station site behind the camera and the photographer standing on the A38 road bridge, No 31145 runs eastbound from Hallen Marsh at 0955 on 2 April 1982, en route to Bristol Parkway to collect a rake of wagons. The bridge and embankment in the distance carry the 1863 route to New Passage Pier. Note the sparse vista ahead and the utilitarian-design building to the right.

Approaching 30 years later, on 11 September 2010, the A38 is a wider and much busier road! The railway scene is vastly altered too, the corridor being encroached upon by tree growth and threatening to swamp the junctions and the end of the 1994 doubled section. The ugly building still stands but, thankfully for aesthetics, is largely hidden by leaves! *Mike Mensing/MJS*

HENBURY: Opened with the line in 1910, the station enjoyed double-track status from 1917 until 1966, by which time it had closed to both passenger traffic and to the freight services that used its twin-siding goods yard. The weather admittedly does not enhance the view, but its appearance on 26 August 1956, looking towards Avonmouth from a passing train, is far from enticing. The coal merchant C. Rudrum & Sons, however, does seem to have a sense of humour, with his 'Here we are again!' slogan.

On a decidedly happier day weather-wise, 54 years later on 11 September 2010, the 'present' view shows the station building and posts for the running-in board still in place but heavily overgrown, while the up platform has completely disappeared. The 1994 doubling is still in place, as traffic from Avonmouth continues to prosper; in 2010 the possibility of biomass trains adding to the coal traffic was under examination. *H. C. Casserley/MJS*

HALLEN MARSH JUNCTION: We are now at the western end of the line from Filton and have joined the Avonmouth to Severn Beach line. On 18 March 1985 Class 121 No B126, coach No W55026, heads north with the 1003 Bristol Temple Meads-Severn Beach local service, passing a railfreight service that awaits the return of its motive power, seen in the distance having run round its train. Note the plethora of pipes and vehicles connected with the various industrial complexes.

It is true that no business can stand still, and this applies both on and off the railway. The railway here has had a third line added and looks in good shape, whereas virtually all the industrial site has changed and only the steep roadway leading to the arrow-straight St Andrews Road is common to both views on 11 September 2010. *Mike Mensing/MJS*

HALLEN MARSH JUNCTION: Viewed from the other side of the road bridge from the previous page, No 47130 slowly reverses its load of just two Polybulk tankers into the Plas Menco siding at 1018 on 18 March 1985. The line curving to the right in the distance is that to Filton, while the track into the middle distance heads for Severn Beach. The 65-lever signal box, opened with the doubling of the Filton line in 1917, closed three years after this view, in 1988.

The former roadway has seen remodelling in recent times, leading to difficulty in precisely reproducing the earlier view. On 11 September 2010 the tracks are still in situ, although scarcely believable, but the signal gantry gives some clue as to the location being railway land! Now long disused, it is unlikely that the rails will again see traffic. With the signal box also absent, and with the appearance of new industrial units, the whole atmosphere is totally different. *Mike Mensing/MJS*

HALLEN MARSH JUNCTION: On 27 April 1982 No 31294 slowly moves south past the junction with a load of tanks. There are chimneys aplenty on the horizon, betraying the industrial presence, but the vista is still an open one at this time. Another Brush product, the 31 was new as D5827 in December 1961, travelling to Sheffield Darnall shed to take up duties. Becoming No 31294 in February 1974, under TOPS, it remained an Eastern Region loco for many years, before spreading its wings. The end came in February 2000, after a period in store. *Tom Heavyside*

Bitton to Bristol Temple Meads (Old)

BITTON: Situated towards the end of the long Midland Railway tentacle that reached out to Bath (Green Park) from Mangotsfield on the Birmingham-Bristol main line, Bitton was the most southerly station of the MR in Gloucestershire. Opened on 4 August 1869, the station was able to offer the whole range of passenger and goods facilities, including handling livestock and horse boxes, and it even boasted a 4-ton crane in the goods yard. On 8 July 1959 the view towards Mangotsfield shows the main building on the down side and the attractive goods shed open for business. The main approach to the station was up a steep road to the right of this view, at a sharp angle to the A431 Bristol-Bath road.

After freight services were withdrawn on 5 July 1965, passenger services only lasted a further eight months, ceasing from 7 March 1966. Happily, the Bristol Suburban Railway Society was determined to ensure that a railway presence survived, and its initial plans were for the line to stretch north from Bitton to eventually regain Yate. Reopening Bitton for visitors from 1977, the group became the Bitton Railway Co Ltd two years later and, subsequently, the Avon Valley Railway. Regaining the track to Oldland Common in 1988, this was to be the northern extremity, as a swelling Bristol swallowed much of the proposed route, and part was subsumed beneath the upgraded A4174 Ring Road. On 14 December 1997 a happy throng of visitors waits for the next arrival, with another visitor, No 9600, in the up platform ready to take over.
Richard Casserley/MJS

BITTON: Looking towards Bath on 10 September 1963, the station is basically being kept neat and tidy but, as seen from a passing train, it has an air of there not being a high patronage. It would appear that the length of platform in most use has been raised slightly and kept free of weeds, whereas the near end seems to have been largely abandoned.

Lunchtime on 24 June 2010 sees a period of inactivity on the preserved Avon Valley Railway, and coaching stock rests in the down platform, necessitating a more constricted comparative view. However, the scene is one of preservation of extant buildings and improvements alongside for the visiting public. The marquee on the left gives cover in the baking heat for the café patrons, still able to obtain refreshments despite the absence of trains; bunting provides a cheerful face; extra seating is on the platform, which is clean, tidy and well cared-for; and the old-style signs add a splash of colour and 'authenticity'. *Colour-Rail collection/MJS*

BITTON: The goods shed (out of view to the right here) still stands in the yard immediately to the north of the station and houses working stock and items awaiting attention. With a 'new' signal box also waiting its turn on the left, No 9600 returns from Oldland Common, having taken the trip north after the view on page 104. *MJS*

Moving north from the station, the line describes a north-easterly arc, squeezing between residential developments. On 13 May 1964 'Standard 3' 2-6-2T No 82037 runs bunker-first as it approaches an overbridge approximately a quarter of a mile north of Bitton, with the 4.30pm Bath Green Park-Bristol Temple Meads local stopping service. Note the Midland Railway notice, tall semaphores and multiplicity of telegraph wires, all features long since lost to the scene. New in April 1955 to South Wales, No 82037 was a much-travelled engine, moving to the Bristol area in 1958 and staying there until withdrawal in September 1965, with just one or two brief 'holidays' elsewhere. *Mike Mensing*

OLDLAND COMMON: Although the MR had been operating over the route since 1869, the station here was not opened until 2 December 1935. Completed to serve a growing suburban development, it was sited in a cutting near to housing and was a cheap affair, with platforms formed of old sleepers and a small ticket office on the footpath leading down to the station. An unstaffed halt in its final years, it was closed, with the rest of the line, on 3 March 1966. The basic nature of the facility can readily be seen in this view from 27 September 1965, looking back towards Bristol from a passing train. Spartan would not be an incorrect description! *H. C. Casserley*

OLDLAND COMMON: The restored railway has had a number of visiting engines over the years but, 20 years from start-up and less than a decade since the line reached this location, 'M7' No 30053 was surely one of the rarest for this line when seen on 14 December 1997, about to return to Bitton. A 1905 member of a class introduced initially in 1897, '53' was one of a number converted for push-pull working from 1925. Its BR life was spent in 'musical chairs' between sheds in the London and Brighton areas before ending its life at Bournemouth on 25 May 1964. Happily, it was spared the cutter's torch, to live again in preservation. Normally based at the Swanage Railway, it was sold to Steamtown Museum in Bellows Falls, Vermont, USA, in 1967, but happily was repatriated in 1987.

As already stated, the railway is prevented from further progress north by encroachment onto the trackbed by Bristol's expansion, as well as the Bristol-Bath footpath/cycleway, so the station remains a quiet backwater of a terminus, with just the single platform and a run-round loop. With the green corridor either side, the lineside walk is now a pleasant affair, as seen on 24 March 2010. *Both MJS*

WARMLEY: A delightful portrait of what pleasure and attractions there were in photographing steam trains. Not only do the loco and train provide interest, but the station furniture, the goods yard and its attendant buildings, and the tasteful architecture cheek-by-jowl with industrial competition all add their pieces to the jigsaw to make this view from the station footbridge one to savour. The wooden waiting room on the down platform is understood to have been the only such wooden structure on the line. No 73140 rushes south through the station with the 1025 Manchester London Road-Bournemouth service, 'The Pines Express', in the late 1950s. *MJS collection*

WARMLEY: Opened on 4 August 1869, with the line, the station was little altered throughout its 97-year career, closing on 3 March 1966, again with the rest of the route. In another attractive view of this location, on 16 October 1965, with less than six months to go, the waiting lady and child are well wrapped up despite the autumn sunshine, but perhaps they were not able to make use of the waiting room, as both wooden buildings look to be out of commission. Smoke still escapes from the brick factory chimney beyond.

With the footbridge no more, following the station closure, the 'present' view is from platform level but at least the platforms are still in situ. The trackbed between Bath and Bristol has been converted into a footpath/cycleway, with some of the past architecture/infrastructure retained. A further attempt at softening the closure blow has been by erecting flat steel 'manikins', representing ghostly staff and passenger 'characters'. A policeman takes a breather from his cycling rounds to watch a different type of motive power on the trackbed on 24 June 2010! Note that the wooden building still stands, now offering food, drink and mementos to the visitor. *Edwin Wilmshurst/MJS*

WARMLEY: In happier times, this MR signal box controlled the railway as it crossed the A420, on the southern entry to the station, but it was left abandoned after closure. By 2 May 1981 it is still in place but now disused and overgrown. With a barbed-wire fence surrounding it and the glass intact in the windows, it is obviously receiving some loving care.

Although in need of a lick of paint and with a bent railing on its former balcony, the signal box has received some redecoration over time, the foliage surrounding it has been cleared and a proper metal railing fence placed around it. On 24 June 2010 one of the two female cyclists turns to look at it, before she and her companion cross the busy road. *Mike Mensing/MJS*

MANGOTSFIELD, unlike the other stations in this section, was a junction, on the eastern point of a triangle. The line to the north-east took trains to Yate and on to Birmingham, south-east to Bath, and westwards to the old Temple Meads station in Bristol. The first station was opened by the MR in 1845, but was replaced by a new structure some half a mile south on 4 August 1869. At its height, there were six platforms, including a bay that handled services to and from Clifton Down. This traffic ceased in 1940, suspended for the war but never reinstated. Passenger services on the Bristol-Yate/Birmingham line (to the left in this view, looking east on 10 September 1963) ended in 1965, and the freight connection to the Lawrence Hill ground frame was removed from 3 January 1970; the south-east route (to the right) closed on 7 March 1966. Traffic on the third, north-south, side of the triangle, which bypassed the station, formally ended in 1962, with the withdrawal of 'The Pines Express', but intermittent, largely freight trains ran for a period thereafter. In the background, Carson's chocolate factory peers over the awnings; it had its own siding until around this time.

Incredibly, on 24 June 2010 the main island platforms remain, with some of the old walls still standing, but the site is now passed by feet and cycle wheels rather than steel ones, as part of pathways to Yate and Bath. A nice touch is the insertion on the platform top of large-scale facsimile tickets from its steam era. *Paul Chancellor collection/MJS*

MANGOTSFIELD: Looking towards Bristol on 4 July 1947, some of the expanse of railway land occupied by the station complex at its height can be gleaned, as the 9.28am Bristol-Gloucester four-coach local arrives. The semaphores, gas lamp, MR notice and signal box all add to the mix, as does the long rake of goods wagons in the right distance, between the two signals. Midland 'Compound' No 1073 (later to become 41073 under BR) was one of the three-cylinder 4P 4-4-0s introduced in 1924 for main-line expresses on the Midland system. Overtaken by more modern designs from the mid-1930s, they still performed useful duties right up to extinction of the class in squadron service. No 1073 was a long-time servant of Bourneville shed (21B), having been resident there for more than a decade at its demise on 7 September 1957.

The view on 24 June 2010 is far more restricted, with land on either side reclaimed by nature and the pathway only requiring minimal width. The Bristol-Bath Railway Path strikes off to the left, with the Ring-Road Path on the right heading to Yate. The sign on the left points weary travellers to The Bridge Inn nearby. *H. C. Casserley/MJS*

MANGOTSFIELD: Moving east along the central island platform, a Stanier Class 3 2-6-2T is espied rumbling into the far left platform with a Bristol-Bath train on 29 April 1950. With the canopies and the hill beyond, there is a slightly unsettling air; indeed, Arnold Ridley obviously felt this, as he wrote his play *The Ghost Train* after being stranded here overnight! In the days of the Travelling Post Office (TPO), the mail-bag-catcher had to be on the left of the train, so mail trains were often turned on the triangle around the station. *H. C. Casserley*

MANGOTSFIELD: These two views from 26 April 1982 show the station after closure. Looking south, the line to Bath arcs away from the photographer, with the route still very clear 15 years or so after track-lifting. The Yate route is in the foreground. Between, the platforms and building walls are still in situ, as is Carson's factory, to the left, and its private cricket ground.

A few yards further east along the hillside, the view concentrates on the Yate route and again shows the wall behind the platform to be in good shape. In 2010 this view was impossible due to the growth and density of invading bushes and trees. The Bristol suburb of Soundwell can be seen through the branches. *Both Ben Ashworth*

FISHPONDS: The first rails through the site appeared in 1835, as part of the railway from Coalpit Heath in the east bringing, appropriately, coal into Bristol. A station was created in March 1866, its early name being Stapleton Halt, but this was quickly changed to Fishponds in July 1867. With the line to Bath from Mangotsfield opening in 1869, then a spur south-west to Clifton Down in 1874, the station was a busy place, but with just two platforms. In addition to goods and passenger facilities, there were a number of sidings, including those for Avonside Locomotive Works (from 1905), Stapleton Road Gas Works and East Bristol Collieries. On 21 July 1957 No 45297 climbs away from the original Temple Meads station, at times on gradients as steep as 1 in 63 before an easing through the station, with the end coaches still on the slope. The station had the distinction of lasting 100 years and 4 days!

This is as close as one can be for a meaningful comparison, as the road alterations in relation to the construction of Morrison's supermarket, to the right, have meant that the trackbed is not strictly followed here by the Bristol & Bath Railway Path. On 2 September 2010, however, the pathway still provides a small oasis of relative peace. *Keith Jones collection, MJS collection/MJS*

FISHPONDS: The same platform is seen again, looking towards Mangotsfield on 26 August 1956, from a train bound for Bristol. Note the rather elaborate chimneys on the typically Midland design of main station building, complete with extensive canopy. Two sidings can just be glimpsed through the bridge. The Clifton Down service was withdrawn in 1941, followed by that to Gloucester from 4 January 1965, and the end came on 7 March 1966 with the closure of the Bath route. Much of the station was razed to the ground in April 1968. As previously stated, the branch to Lawrence Hill ground frame closed in January 1970.

Again, the precise alignment of the railway has been lost due to road alterations; indeed, the old road bridge has been replaced by a fresh design, which can just be seen in the distance as both the trajectory and gradient of the footpath deviate from the erstwhile railway. However, on 1 September 2010 part of the site and name is marked by the imaginative sculpture – showing a fish trying to find its pond? *H. C. Casserley/ MJS*

FISHPONDS: Seen from the station signal box in April 1962, looking towards Bristol and the final stretch of the climb from Temple Meads, Midland 4F 0-6-0 No 44135 breathes an almost audible sigh of relief approaching Fishponds station with empty coaching stock for an evening postal service, apparently en route to Mangotsfield for turning. The box closed exactly six years later. There are turnouts into sidings on both sides of the operating lines and a derelict old signal box. On this down side there was a waiting shelter, smaller than the main building but still with pitched roof and chimney, to the rear of which were large industrial works for many years. *A. E. Durrant,John Chalcraft Collection*

BRISTOL BARROW ROAD SHED: As with any railway entrance to a large town or city in steam days, especially where there was a terminus, there was need for an engine shed, to coal, water and sometimes turn the locomotives that had worked in. For spotters, these were Mecca, especially on Sundays, when large gatherings of the monsters could be observed at close hand. Looking north towards the eponymous Barrow Road bridge, top left, we see the former Midland facility serving Bristol on 3 October 1964. With the Digby Street terraced housing giving accommodation for some of the shed workers, BR Standard 9F No 92000 stands in company with ex-LMS and GWR locos, including, of the latter, Nos 6958 *Oxburgh Hall* and 7022 *Hereford Castle*. *Ben Ashworth*

BRISTOL BARROW ROAD SHED: As already seen, despite being an ex-LMS shed the appearance of GWR locomotives was certainly not unknown. In September 1965 No 6859 *Yiewsley Grange* has been turned and prepared for its return to South Wales, as the ex-GWR (Bath Road) shed had closed to steam as far back as 1960. With just three months before the end of steam throughout the BR(W) system, and two before this loco's withdrawal, the nameplates and even their brackets have disappeared and it wears a non-standard numberplate on the smokebox front. To the left, beyond the young spotter, another 'Grange' stands forlorn. Note the three gabled and slated pitched roofs covering the square roundhouse.

A once familiar Bristol landmark, these two gas holders stand in the background of both views. Nos 48253, of Mold Junction shed, stands alongside the shed building together with former Crosti-boilered 9F No 92028. While these two and the accompanying 4F 0-6-0 are all in steam on 3 July 1965, the line of ex-GWR pannier tanks to the right are not! One of the Stanier 8Fs to return from war service in 1949, No 48253 was a much-travelled loco, but usually remaining around the Crewe, Chester and Liverpool areas. *Ben Ashworth/John Chalcraft*

BRISTOL BARROW ROAD SHED: All railways have need of smaller engines, which can handle more menial tasks such as shunting stock or handling short-haul duties, whether freight or passenger, and cope with tight curves. On 18 March 1956 No 41879 stands in the yard's throat, close to Barrow Road bridge, between calls to move stock around the shed. An unidentified 'Jubilee' prepares to move under the bridge. One of Johnson's 1878-designed 1F 0-6-0Ts, No 41879 was later rebuilt with a Belpaire firebox, as seen here. Having worked around Birmingham for many years, it was transferred to Bristol in March 1955, where it stayed until withdrawal on 26 March 1960.

Just four months later, on 15 July 1956, the photographer and No 73002 (from Nottingham) were both visitors to the shed, whereas No 44537 is on home ground. It would stay here until October 1959, then would begin a long trail north and east, first to Warrington for a month, thence to Carnforth and finally to Leeds Holbeck shed. Its end was on 3 November 1962. Barrow Road shed opened in 1873 and possessed all the major features required by such a large and busy location. Improvements to coal and ash plants (just visible on the right) came in 1938, but they were to serve for less than 30 years, the shed closing on 20 November 1965. *Gerald Adams, MJS collection/H. C. Casserley*

BRISTOL BARROW ROAD SHED: In another part of the yard on 18 March 1956 two more examples of smaller workhorses stand temporarily idle. Another of Johnson's 1Fs is in company with a more modern and slightly more powerful side tank, 'Jinty' No 47552. Once a Midlands loco, it came to Barrow Road in January 1953 and stayed until May 1962, with a brief spell at Templecombe (October 1959-January 1960), before returning to Templecombe as its final home, with withdrawal coming on 26 January 1963.

Following closure in 1965, the shed buildings were demolished and the whole of the sizeable location redeveloped into industrial use. Thus in 2010 it is virtually impossible to accurately replicate vantage points and there is precious little that can even be identified as ex-railway. On 2 September 2010, however, a boundary wall still stands, as demarcation for the Bristol & Bath Railway Path, and this is seen standing defiantly between the twin industrial developments. *Gerald Adams, MJS collection/MJS*

AVONSIDE WHARF: At the lower end of the MR's incursion into GWR territory in Bristol, a freight handling operation was set up at Avonside Wharf. With Bristol Temple Meads in the background, No 08643 shunts the cement sidings at the Wharf on 13 May 1984. New from Horwich Works in January 1959 and allocated to Newport, first to Pill and then Ebbw Junction sheds, it has basically remained a 'Western' engine for its whole life, still being around into 2010.

Slightly later in the day No 08643 grumbles up the Avonside Wharf branch with the tank wagons seen in the picture above. Note the wall on the left, so reminiscent of Barrow Road's boundary. The area to the left, by the stop blocks, has now become Barrow Road Waste Depot. *Both John Chalcraft*

BRISTOL (MR): We are now approaching the end of our journey, but on 3 July 1965 No 7912 *Little Linford Hall* travels in the opposite direction as it takes the Midland line out of Bristol Temple Meads and prepares to pass what would become Barton Hill depot, with 1M35 for the Midlands. Again the date is significant, as it is less than six months to the end of steam for the GWR locos that had not been transferred to sheds now in the Midland Region. No 7912 bears the scar, being without nameplates and shedplate, and having a hastily applied unofficial front numberplate.

On the same day, a couple of hundred yards closer to our goal, ex-GWR 0-6-0PT No 9680 reverses back towards Bristol Barrow Road having finished its duties at Temple Meads station. A servant of Barrow Road since February 1965, it was to last until the end of the year and the dispensing of steam by BR(W). It was a relatively young loco, being new to Tyseley in May 1949, and had travelled widely, being allocated at various times to St Blazey, Swindon and Worcester. *Both John Chalcraft*

BRISTOL TEMPLE MEADS (OLD): Initially designed by I. K. Brunel as the terminus for trains from London, the station was built to his 7ft 0¼in broad gauge, leading to a wide, spacious structure. Opened in 1840, it was quickly being used by the Great Western, Bristol & Exeter and Bristol & Gloucester railways, but this volume of traffic was to change following the opening of the 'new' Temple Meads through station in 1845 and its subsequent development and enlargement. Passenger services to Gloucester (along the old Midland route) ceased in 1965 and the original terminal platforms formally closed on 12 September of that year. Just two months before, on 3 July, 'Standard 3' 2-6-2T No 82038 leaves with a service for Bath Green Park. The less than pristine appearance of the loco matches the feeling of abandonment that was approaching the terminus itself. To the right, the lines to Wapping Wharf, via Redcliffe Viaduct and Tunnel, are still in place, although the connection along the Bristol Harbour branch had closed on 6 January 1964.

The mouth of Brunel's design looks suitably imposing as a setting for a long-distance departure. On 1 September 1962, with the clock fast approaching 4.45pm, No 44776, on the 1M24 working to the Midlands, slowly starts to leave with a good head of steam to take it north to Birmingham. Allocated to Saltley, Birmingham (21A), it had been shedded there for nigh on nine years by this date, but would move a month later to Derby, then Leicester, back to Saltley, Tyseley, Birkenhead and finally Wigan. *John Chalcraft/Ben Ashworth*

BRISTOL TEMPLE MEADS (OLD): Further inside, the train shed could look a little gloomy, but this was counteracted by the magnificence of Brunel's design. The long platforms were split into two, with Nos 12 and 13 this side and 14 and 15 across the tracks. The sepulchral interior is seen on 17 October 1965, still looking operational despite the last train having left the previous month. The left-hand pillars led to an exit from the station. Note the later style of 'Cafeteria & Bar' sign compared to its neighbours.

The view on 4 September 2010 shows the truncating of the overall shed roof since the end of services, that the pillars are gated and the main body of the station is now a car park, a status it has held since shortly after closure. Sadly, although this end has benefited from repainting, the inside of the shed now feels neglected, with abundant pigeon droppings throughout. *John Edgington/MJS*

INDEX OF LOCATIONS

BRISTOL TEMPLE MEADS (OLD): With 'Bristol Old Station Signal Box' to the right – closed on 12 September 1965, with the station – another Stanier 'Black 5' stands with a short rake of coaching stock in the depths of the station. Blowing off, with plenty of steam available, No 44825 prepares to draw forward under Brunel's mock hammer-beam roof into Platform 12 with a stopping train for Gloucester on 7 September 1963. The left-hand sign points the way to the subway to reach the far platforms. This section is now partitioned, for alternative use, which included the British Empire & Commonwealth Museum until 2008. At the time of writing, the area is still closed to the public. *Ben Ashworth*